THE DARK, CLOSE WOOD:

THE WILDERNESS, ELLWOOD,
AND THE BATTLE THAT REDEFINED BOTH

by Chris Mackowski

Design and production by Jackson Foster, The ID Entity, Fredericksburg, Virginia

To Heidi, who was always there for me when I came out of the Wilderness.

ACKNOWLEDGEMENTS

First, I thank John Hennessy for asking me to write this book. It was an immensely gratifying experience. I also thank Greg Mertz, the man who first opened my eyes to this oft-overlooked and underappreciated battle, and Kris White, who spent many hours with me tromping across the battlefield.

Eric Mink, Noel Harrison, and Don Pfanz provided materials and research assistance that were absolutely critical to this volume. Don also offered invaluable editorial assistance. I am deeply indebted to each of them and am fortunate to have them as friends.

I also thank Josef Rokus for his contributions on the civilians of the Wilderness, and Carolyn Elstner for her background information on Ellwood. Thanks, too, to Janice Frye, Joe Obidzinski, Fran Smith, and Frank O'Reilly.

Gordon Rhea's book *The Battle of the Wilderness: May 5-6, 1864* is not only the most exhaustive study of the battle, it's also highly readable. Mr. Rhea's book was profoundly inspiring to me as a writer. He writes history the way it's meant to be written.

At St. Bonaventure University's Russell J. Jandoli of Journalism and Mass Communication, I thank the dean, Lee Coppola, and Professor Patrick Vecchio for their continued support. Professor Carole McNall, who has explored the battlefield with me, provided useful lawerly advice. I also offer a special tip of the hat to my colleague John Hanchette, an ardent supporter of battlefield preservation efforts.

Additional thanks go to Jackson Foster of The ID Entity for his design work and his enthusiasm. It is such a pleasure to work with him on this series. Thanks, too, to Nathan Funke for his work colorizing the historical sketch used on the cover and to Lauren Ruffini and Megan Sorokes for the extra editing. I am also indebted to Alex and Kathy Hartley, who pinch-hit in valuable ways that allowed me to do much of the research and photography for this book.

Lastly, and most importantly, I thank Heidi and my kids, Stephanie and Jackson, for letting me spend so much time in the Wilderness. I was glad to always have someone waiting for me when I came out.

CONTENTS

FOREWORD

Wilderness. Today that word has a far different meaning than
it did to nineteenth-century Americans. To us, wilderness is a
preserve, a refuge far away from modern noise and confusion,
a place to recreate and re-create the spirit. In the nineteenth
century, wilderness meant a place that had not yet been
properly civilized, a place needing to be tamed by plow and
structure. In fact, many religious people considered the wilderness Satan's domain. Surely, those who went through the
hellish experience of battle in the Wilderness in 1864 would
have agreed.

Each battle of the Civil War has its own particular "per-
sonality," the aspect that came to define it in its own time and
thereafter. At Fredericksburg, it is the hopeless charges against
the Sunken Road with its impregnable stone wall. At Spotsylvania, it is the Bloody Angle with the most deadly hand-to-hand
combat of the war. At the Battle of the Wilderness, the name
of the battle itself is its defining feature. Darkness, confusion,
fire, smoke, separation from comrades, and death from an
unseen source characterize the battle.

Soldiers persevered in a back-and-forth chaotic struggle
filled with horrors. Most marched away from the bloody stale-
mate to other battles, but many were left behind where they
had fallen. No doubt, some of those brave soldiers are still
claimed by the Wilderness. There was no time for organized
burial parties after the battle. The first organized effort at
burial took place more than a year later. By then, remains were
scattered and hidden in the dense thickets of the Wilderness.

No veteran could forget the Wilderness, nor did they want
their descendents to forget what happened here. In 1927
Congress set aside part of the Wilderness Battlefield for all
time as part of Fredericksburg & Spotsylvania National
Military Park. Since then the park has grown to include
almost half of the area where the most intense fighting took
place. Within the park stands the sole surviving structure to
witness (and participate in) the battle, Ellwood Manor.

Today, thanks to a partnership between the Friends of Wilderness Battlefield (FoWB) and the National Park Service, Ellwood has been restored to its Civil War appearance. Inside the house, exhibits and FoWB interpreters keep alive the story of both the Wilderness community and the Battle of the Wilderness.

The National Park Service is making other improvements to help the battlefield tell its story. Additions include the Vermont Monument, an artillery piece, a trail, pull-offs and wayside signs. The fine publication by Chris Mackowski that you are now reading joins those efforts to help park visitors attain an overall understanding and appreciation of the incredible story of courage and sacrifice that unfolded amidst a "dark, close wood."

Russell P. Smith
Superintendent
Fredericksburg & Spotsylvania NMP

"What a curse war is. The dreadful sights I have seen this week in this Wilderness will never be banished from my memory. The woods are on fire in various places and horrible to think of hundreds of wounded men are in danger of being roasted alive. I am more than ever convinced that those who were instrumental in bringing the curse of this cruel war upon the country have committed an unpardonable crime against humanity which deserves not only the maledictions of mankind, but likewise the anathemas of an offended God."

Alex Boteler, member of Jeb Stuart's staff

Diary entry for Saturday, May 7, 1864

ELLWOOD:
THE PRESENT AS PROLOGUE

—————

**Today, Ellwood looks much
as it did in the 19th Century.**

It's quiet there now in the simple frame house. No cannons boom. No muskets roar. No wounded cry for help.

No children laugh in the dooryard as they run and play.

No cattle low. No horses whinny.

No song drifts up from around the fire pit in front of the slave cabins.

Instead, a blue-tailed skink suns itself on the stone steps that lead up to the front porch, which looks out over the Wilderness Run valley. Once, a driveway looped up to the foot of the steps from the Parker's Store Road, but both the driveway and the road have disappeared. Now visitors, when they come, approach from the back along a thin ribbon of gravel driveway that cuts across a cornfield from modern Route 20.

The house has stood perched on the hilltop since the 1790s, surrounded on all sides by hundreds of acres of cultivated land. On the edge of the fields looms the remains of a forest that was once part of a larger, forbidding region known as the Wilderness. The house stood as an oasis in the middle of a dark, close wood.

In all the centuries it stood there, just two families ever owned the house. Many other families lived on the plantation, too—black families—but as property, not as owners.

They have all passed into the history of this place.

The trace of the old carriage lane still leads up the hill to Ellwood's front door.

The old catalpa tree that once grew in front of the house made it into the twenty-first century before it, too, finally passed into history. A seedling from that tree now grows in its place, and two other catalpas flank the old carriage entrance. There are maples and cedars and sycamores and a quartet of Kentucky coffee trees. The wind rustles their leaves. Birds chirp in their branches. They might be the only sounds on some days.

On others, visitors can climb the front steps—sending the skink scurrying for the safety of its lair in one of the cracks between the stones—and go inside. Boot heels clunk on the wooden floors and echo off the walls.

There's the sound of friendly chatter. The sound of memories.

The sound of stories being told.

CHAPTER ONE
ELLWOOD

William Jones built
Ellwood in the mid-1790s.
It would remain in his family
into the twentieth century.

They paid £30 a year to live in the middle of the wide, wild woods—an area so wild it had earned the name "the Wilderness." It was the Virginia frontier.

William and Betty Jones had come there to the edge of Spotsylvania County, in part, because the colony's most desirable land, along the Virginia Tidewater, had all been gobbled up. The interior of the colony, while perhaps not quite so inviting, at least offered the hope of better things to come. Pioneers had trickled into the region as early as 1714, when then-Governor Alexander Spotswood actively cultivated settlement, but the population remained sparse. The Wilderness, as a place to live, had never really caught on.

But sometime in the early 1770s William and Betty and William's brother and sister-in-law, Churchill and Judith, separated themselves from their wealthy Tidewater family and moved to the Wilderness to live on land leased from Spotswood's heirs. The four of them toiled and tilled and made lives for themselves until, in 1788, William had collected enough to buy a chunk of property outright—£600 for 642 acres. Churchill, who had gone off to serve in the Continental Army, returned from the Revolution to set up a home, Woodville, on an adjoining parcel. The two brothers dined together four nights a week until Churchill's death in 1822.

By the mid-1790s, William began work on a two-story frame house that sat atop a long ridge overlooking the Wilderness Run valley. He called the house Ellwood, although

By 1830, William Jones had acquired five thousand acres for his plantation. His home, Ellwood, can be seen in the distance in the center of the photo.

the name also shows up in various records as "Elwood" and "Elkwood." The house served as the hub of a successful agricultural operation that grew corn, wheat, and oats. The property also boasted stables, barns, an outdoor kitchen, and cabins to house the 100 slaves that worked the land. A small family cemetery stood a few hundred yards south of the house. Several venerable trees graced the dooryard.

Over time, Jones became one of the wealthiest men in the county. Aside from the money he made from his agricultural holdings, he collected income from timber he sold as fuel to the local iron furnaces and collected rent from the Wilderness Tavern, which he built near the edge of his property along the turnpike that ran between Fredericksburg and Orange Court House.

Jones also added to his wealth by adding to his property, acquiring tracts of 100 acres, 253 acres, 910 acres. By 1830, the entire Ellwood plantation totaled five thousand acres, worth $17,878. Compared to other antebellum plantations, Ellwood was pretty typical; compared to other homesteads

scattered throughout the Wilderness, though, Ellwood seemed huge. The four hundred acres of cleared, cultivated land—identified as "improved" land on the tax rolls—was four times larger than the average in the South for the time.

As one of the most prominent estates between Fredericksburg and Orange Court House, Ellwood frequently hosted guests. Revolutionary War hero "Light Horse" Harry Lee—father of Confederate General Robert E. Lee—supposedly stayed in one of the upstairs rooms and wrote his memoirs. Another hero of the Revolution, the Marquis de Lafayette, dined at the house during his 1825 tour of America. Presidents James Madison and James Monroe may have also visited the house.

In 1823, on a trip to Richmond, Betty Jones died. Five years later, the 78-year-old Jones married 16-year-old Lucinda Gordon, his first wife's grandniece. In 1829, they had a daughter, whom they named Betty Churchill after Jones's first wife.

When Jones died in 1845, Lucinda inherited Ellwood—but only for the duration of her widowhood. If she remarried,

The Wilderness Tavern, built by William Jones along the Orange Turnpike.

Betty Churchill Jones, daughter of William Jones and wife of James Horace Lacy.

she had to forfeit her claim on the estate, which she did in 1847. The following year, she moved to her new husband's home, Greenwood, in Orange County and her daughter, Betty, took formal possession of Ellwood.

That same year, Betty married J. Horace Lacy, a lawyer and educator. Lacy was "broken down aristocracy," said one local resident, fine looking and with a good education but no funds. Betty, a haughty woman who reportedly said that she'd prefer to see the Devil walk up to her gate rather than a poor person, married Lacy anyway. "[A]fter he married her," said the local, "he became the lion of the Wilderness." The Lacys would eventually have eight children spaced over seventeen years.

In 1857, the Lacys bought a grand manor in Fredericksburg called Chatham, which sat atop the bluffs overlooking the Rappahannock River. Chatham had once belonged to Betty's uncle Churchill and her father, William, but despite the family connection, their enthusiasm for the move, said Horace, was "softened down a little now by the thought that we must leave dear old Ellwood."

The Lacys did hold on to Ellwood, though, using it as a summer home, and life there continued much as it always had: till, plant, tend, and harvest. The goods were then shipped east to Fredericksburg and sold at market.

But in 1861, war rumbled across Virginia. Lacy, an ardent secessionist, joined the Confederate army, eventually working his way up to major. Betty, meanwhile, moved with her four children into the home of a friend in Fredericksburg. At Ellwood, operations continued under the supervision of a Mr. Jones—no relation to Betty's father—and a "skeleton force of slaves." Lacy had sent most of his slaves to a plantation he rented near the James River hoping the location, far removed from the fighting, would keep them secure.

At first, war only brushed Ellwood: a minor skirmish in late April 1863 as Confederates tried to delay the Union army's advance toward Chancellorsville. When the battle erupted, though, and wounded soldiers flooded to the rear, Ellwood became a field hospital.

At another nearby field hospital, the battle's most notable casualty, Confederate Lieutenant General Thomas Jonathan "Stonewall" Jackson, had his left arm amputated. Jackson's chaplain, Beverley Tucker Lacy—Horace's brother—brought Jackson's arm to the Lacy family cemetery for burial.

Left: Churchill Jones.
Right: William Jones.

Shortly thereafter, Jones took Lacy's remaining slaves to the James River plantation, leaving Ellwood deserted.

In November, the two armies moved back into the area and faced off along Mine Run, seven miles to the west of Ellwood. As the Federal army marched by the plantation, soldiers ransacked the house, targeting, in particular, Lacy's library.

Nevertheless, Ellwood managed to weather these disruptions—troubles that would prove mild compared to what the war had yet to bring.

The Arm

During a rare quiet moment during the Battle of the Wilderness, probably sometime on May 7, an engineering officer from New York spent some time walking the grounds at Ellwood.

The granite monument that marks the burial spot of Stonewall Jackson's arm was placed in the Lacy family cemetery in 1903 by James Power Smith. Smith, formerly of Jackson's staff, married the Lacys' eldest daughter, Agnes.

I was much interested and impressed on approaching a common looking farm house situated in an opening in the woods, to learn that Stonewall Jackson was buried near by.

His grave was situated in the heart of the Wilderness on a knoll, unmarked by stone or board. It was hard to realize, as I stood beside that lonely grave, that the little mound of earth before me hid from view all that was mortal of the man whose great deeds had filled the world with wonder and amazement... I lingered for a long time at the grave of that wonderful and eccentric man.

Nor could I leave the spot without having experienced those peculiar feelings of awe and respect for the memory of the genius which, though that of an enemy, possessed the faculty which inspired his Soldiers with a religious enthusiasm, resulting in most wonderful victories and made his name a terror to ourselves.

The Union officer incorrectly believed that Jackson himself was buried at Ellwood, but in fact, only Jackson's arm had been interred there following its amputation in May 1863.

The general himself lay buried miles away, near his home in Lexington, Virginia. Nevertheless, the arm, now marked by a small monument erected in 1903, evokes Jackson's presence, and even today it remains a point of interest for those who visit the property.

CHAPTER TWO

THE WILDERNESS

Several tributaries of Wilderness Run snaked their way through the low-lying areas of the forest.

For seventy square miles, the undulating hills were awash in trees—"a vast sea" of dense forest, wrote one visitor.

Another described the region less kindly as "one of the waste places of nature." "It is a region of gloom and the shadow of death," said another. Someone even likened it to "the wildest regions of Dante's 'Inferno.'"

This was the Wilderness, a thick second-growth forest that sprawled across the rolling terrain of central Virginia. The hills themselves, like choppy waves, rose and fell and broke in all directions. The forest, thick and vibrant, laid claim to everything else.

It was young, as forests go. Once, magnificent stands of timber grew on the hills. But settlers found iron ore, abundant in the region, in the early 1700s. By 1718, the first of several iron furnaces opened to smelt the ore and process it for export. Those furnaces, of course, needed fuel; some could burn as much as 750 acres' worth of timber in a year. To provide that fuel, furnace owners clear-cut much of the region's trees.

In the wake of that clear-cutting, a second-growth forest sprung up—a dense growth of scrubby pines and whiplash oaks, briars and thorn bushes, vines and ivies and creepers, honeysuckle, and wild roses. "You had a tangle through which a dog could hardly force its way," said one man.

A few streams wound their way among the hills, and the depressions in the terrain hid wet, marshy spots. "The scrawny, moss-tagged pines, the garroted alders, the

Todd's Tavern provided one of the few way stations for travelers heading through the vast Wilderness.

hoary willows," said one visitor, "gives a very sad look to these wet thickets."

A macadamized turnpike ran through the heart of the Wilderness, stretching east toward Fredericksburg and west toward Orange Court House. A second road, the Orange Plank Road, which got its name from the timber planks used as paving, also twisted through the area. Few other good roads traversed the region, "only a labyrinth of wagon tracks and bridle paths leading to and from the river to the furnaces and clearings of the settlers," according to one traveler.

Indeed, as inhospitable as the Wilderness seemed, a few families eked out livings by farming small patches cut out of the forest. Some owned slaves, although many were too poor.

Residents had a store, Parker's Store, which sat along the Orange Plank Road. They also had the Wilderness Church, built around 1853 along Orange Turnpike, to meet their spiritual needs. A few miles to the west of the church sat the Wilderness Tavern, where the stagecoach stopped. Travelers heading southwest toward Orange Court House could also stop at Robertson's Tavern or, if heading south toward Spotsylvania Court House, at Todd's Tavern. If heading east toward Fredericksburg, travelers could seek lodging at the tavern at the Chancellorsville crossroads.

In the spring of 1863, war swept through the Wilderness. The Army of the Potomac, in an attempt to slip behind the Confederate Army of Northern Virginia, which was hunkered down in a nearly impregnable position in Fredericksburg some twelve miles to the east, marched into the Wilderness from the north and west. The Confederates discovered the Federal maneuver in time and intercepted the larger army just as it was forging eastward from Chancellorsville. The resulting battle left thirty thousand casualties in its wake. Many who died were buried where they fell—or never buried at all.

Taken along the Orange Plank Road, this postwar photo shows "the close, dark wood" of the Wilderness crowding in on either side.

When the armies again converged on the Wilderness a year later, the forest gave up those dead. Union soldiers, camping near the Chancellorsville intersection, found the bones of fallen comrades washed out of their shallow graves or dug up by wild animals. "The dead horses had dwindled away to bones and the dead men to bones and underclothing," wrote one soldier. "I found a dozen skulls in twice as many rods travel and could doubtless have found scores by a little examination of the thick underbrush."

"This, viewed as a battleground, was simply infernal," a Union soldier later said.

When the Union army returned to the Wilderness in May of 1864, they found the exposed remains of hundreds of soldiers who had died at the Battle of Chancellorsville the previous spring.

Major General Andrew Humphreys, chief of staff for Army of the Potomac commander Major General George G. Meade, planned the Union army's route through the Wilderness. Humphreys planned to move through the area as quickly as possible but Meade chose to stop overnight in order to let the Federal army's wagon train catch up.

The thick foliage of the Wilderness made the country nearly impenetrable. There was little room for cavalry to operate, artillery to deploy, or large bodies of men to maneuver. "It is impossible to conceive a field worse adapted to the movements of a grand army," wrote a Union officer. "A more unpromising theatre of war was never seen," said another.

Lieutenant General Ulysses S. Grant, commander of all Union armies, saw the Wilderness as a formidable obstacle that stood between the Army of the Potomac and the Army of Northern Virginia. The ground offered no possibility for drawing Lee's army out into open combat. "All the conditions were favorable for defensive operations," Grant noted.

Grant had almost 119,000 men at his disposal, and although he didn't know Lee's strength—the Confederates had 65,000 men available—Grant felt confident in his numerical superiority. "[I]t was my intention to fight Lee between Culpeper and Richmond if he would stand," Grant later wrote.

But first, the Army of the Potomac had to get through the Wilderness as quickly as possible and into the open country beyond. Only then could Grant bring his numerical superiority to bear.

And so, beginning on May 3, 1864, the Union army began to thaw after its long winter of dormancy. Roads, like dry riverbeds, suddenly filled with a rush of blue as the Army of the Potomac flowed south, over the Rapidan River and into the heart of the most inhospitable terrain the army had ever occupied.

The Wilderness, unruly, interminable, and still haunted by the failures of the previous year, pressed in on all sides. "It was," said one of Grant's closest aides, "a wilderness in the most forbidding sense of the word."

The Union army entered the Wilderness by crossing at Germanna Ford. To avoid a bottleneck, a smaller wing of the army crossed at Ely's Ford, a few miles farther east.

A Deserted Waste

A correspondent from the *Philadelphia Inquirer* described the
Wilderness in an article widely reproduced across the north:

*The word wilderness conveys generally the impression of
a deserted waste; and the term, applied to the region in which
the great battle was fought, was no misnomer. It is an exceed-
ingly broken table land, irregular in its confirmation and so
densely covered with dwarf timber and undergrowth, as to ren-
der progress through it very difficult and laborious off the few
roads and paths that penetrate it. The timber was so effectually
[an ally] of the rebels, for they had taken care to take position
near its edge, leaving us an open country at our back, so that
a whole division drawn up in battle might be invisible a few
hundred feet off.*

Catharine Furnace

Charles Wellford, owner of Catharine Furnace.

The last iron furnace to operate in the region was Catharine Furnace. Built in 1837, the furnace operated for a decade before shutting down. At the start of the war, it reopened, and despite attempts by Brigadier General George Armstrong Custer's Federal cavalry to shut it down in May 1864, it produced iron for the Confederacy until the war's end.

Catharine Furnace could produce approximately two tons of processed iron for every acre of timber it burned, and it could burn through about one hundred acres per year—modest compared to the capacity of some furnaces, which could burn through as much as 750 acres annually.

It took between sixty and seventy laborers—mostly slaves—to dig the ore, cut the timber, haul the materials, and operate the furnace, which usually ran for four or five months at a time. Workers dumped cartloads of raw ore down the open maw of the furnace tower, where the temperature reached 2,800 degrees. The ore would melt, workers would separate the impurities from the molten iron, and the resulting slag was skimmed off and hauled away. Workers would then pour the remaining iron into molds to create bars, called "pigs," that would then be sent elsewhere for further refinement.

Aside from the furnace itself, the facility encompassed six to ten other buildings and more than forty-six hundred acres.

Today, the furnace's large stack, standing thirty-six feet tall, is all that remains of the once-bustling and vital industry that helped give the Wilderness its distinctive character.

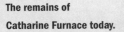

The remains of Catharine Furnace today.

CHAPTER THREE

GRANT TAKES CONTROL

Lieutenant General
Ulysses S. Grant, commander
of all Union armies.

The pile of wood shavings at his feet had grown steadily throughout the afternoon.

Across the Orange Turnpike, next to the Lacy house, Union artillery maintained a near-constant barrage aimed at the Confederates somewhere farther to the west. Somewhere else, the muffled sound of rifle fire tried to push its way through thick underbrush. Couriers raced into headquarters on horseback, delivered the scribbled messages entrusted to their care, then raced away with fresh orders.

Ulysses S. Grant paid little heed to any of it. He hardly even paid attention to the penknife he held in his right glove as he sliced away strip after thin strip of wood from the stick he held in his left. When he worked one stick into shavings, he picked up another and started anew. The whittling, said an aide, played "sad havoc" on the gloves, which had several holes peeled into them.

"It was amusing," said an observer, "to see him—the Commander-in-Chief—whittling away with his knife upon the bark of a tree, pausing now and then to throw in a word or sentence in the conversation of those grouped about, and then going to work again with renewed vigor upon the incision of the pine."

The observer, a newspaper correspondent who had traveled with Grant in Mississippi and Tennessee, knew the general well. "[B]ut as I strolled thro' the group of officers reclining under the trees at headquarters, I looked for him

On seeing Grant, one reporter wrote: "[T]he plain, quiet man who sat with his back against a tree, apparently heedless and unmoved, was the one on whom the fortunes of the day, if not of the age and country, were hanging."

When Grant rode with his army into the Wilderness, his men were eager to see what their new commander was made of.

some time in vain, such was his insignificant, unpretending aspect and conduct while the battle was raging in all its fury," the reporter admitted. He thought a stranger to headquarters "would have little dreamed that the plain, quiet man who sat with his back against a tree, apparently heedless and unmoved, was the one on whom the fortunes of the day, if not of the age and country, were hanging."

As he whittled, he smoked cigars. On bad days, like today, he might go through as many as twenty of them. If he felt particularly stressed, the puffs of smoke popped from the cigar's end more feverishly, more frequently, but otherwise, said a staff officer, Grant maintained an "imperturbability of countenance."

He had come from the West, this quiet, unassuming man, and he was unlike anything the Army of the Potomac had seen before. They were used to the showiness of George McClellan, the good-natured but martial Ambrose Burnside, the hard-edged bluster of "Fighting Joe" Hooker, the booming temper of George Gordon Meade.

Grant, on the other hand, had "a good deal of rough dignity," said one Federal. Another described him as "stumpy, unmilitary, slouchy, and Western-looking; very ordinary in fact."

"There is no enthusiasm in the army for Gen. Grant," said a colonel from Maine; "and, on the other hand, there is no prejudice against him. We are prepared to throw up our hats for him when he shows himself the great soldier here in Virginia against Lee and the best troops of the rebels."

Grant had earned a reputation as "the great soldier" out west, but that held little sway with the men of the Army of the Potomac. "Well, Grant has never met Bobby Lee yet," Federal soldiers said to each other.

Nonetheless, they could not deny that Grant had won important victories at Forts Henry and Donelson and at Shiloh. In a fit of jealousy over the successes, his own superior, Major General Henry Halleck, tried to "retire" him, but President Lincoln himself had recalled Grant from exile. "I can't spare this man," Lincoln said. "He fights." Grant repaid the president's confidence by winning a crucial victory at

Executive Mansion
Washington, April 30, 1864

Lieutenant General Grant:

Not expecting to see you again before the Spring campaign opens, I wish to express, in this way, my entire satisfaction with what you have done up to this time, so far as I understand it. The particulars of your plans I neither know, or seek to know. You are vigilant and self-reliant; and, pleased with this, I wish not to obtrude any constraints or restraints upon you. While I am very anxious that any great disaster, or the capture of our men in great numbers, shall be avoided, I know these points are less likely to escape your attention than they would be mine. If there is anything wanting which is within my power to give, do not fail to let me know it.

And now with a brave Army, and a just cause, may God sustain you.

Yours very truly
A. Lincoln.

Just days before Grant opened the Overland Campaign, President Lincoln wrote to express his "entire satisfaction" with his new commander.

Vicksburg and then crossing Tennessee to save the Union army trapped in Chattanooga.

In the East, meanwhile, the Army of the Potomac had achieved a major victory at Gettysburg, but the army commander, Major General George Gordon Meade, let the Confederates escape without a vigorous pursuit. In the months afterward, Meade's greatest success may have been that he hadn't lost a major engagement—but he hadn't managed to be in one, either. Like his predecessors, Meade seemed content to avoid a pitched battle with Lee.

So Lincoln brought Grant east.

Lincoln didn't want Grant to command just a single army, though. Instead, he promoted Grant to lieutenant general—a rank not awarded to a U.S. military commander since George Washington—and he placed Grant in charge of all Federal armies. "You are vigilant and self-reliant," Lincoln told him; "and, pleased with this, I wish not to obtrude any constraints or restraints upon you."

Major General George Gordon Meade, commander of the Union Army of the Potomac.

Lincoln believed he had finally found a general who understood the grim math of war and who possessed the resolve to do what needed to be done, as unpleasant as it would be.

Grant believed no peace could be possible with the South "until the military power of the rebellion was entirely broken." So far, the Confederacy had thwarted Federal attempts at breaking that military power despite the fact that "the resources of the enemy and his numerical strength were far inferior to ours."

The answer, Grant believed, was "to hammer continuously against the armed force of the enemy and his resources, until by mere attrition, if in no other way, there should be nothing left to him…."

To achieve this, Grant developed a grand strategy that would mobilize all Federal armies in concert with one another —something never before attempted during the war. The coordinated movement would allow him "to use the greatest number of troops practicable against the armed forces of the enemy, preventing him from using the same force at different seasons against first one and then another of our armies…."

He ordered his friend and confidant, Major General William Tecumseh Sherman, to move south from Tennessee toward Atlanta, Georgia. He ordered Major General Nathaniel Banks to move from New Orleans toward Mobile, Alabama. In Virginia, he ordered Major General Franz Sigel to move up the Shenandoah Valley and Major General Benjamin Butler to move up the Peninsula toward Richmond. Meanwhile, Meade was to take the Army of the Potomac and engage Lee's Army of Northern Virginia. "Lee's army will be your objective," Grant told Meade. "Wherever Lee goes, there you will go also."

And Grant, too, would go. He announced his intention to make his office not back in Washington but in the field with Meade's army. In deference, Meade offered to resign, but Grant assured him his services were needed. Grant planned to tell Meade what he wanted done and leave it to Meade to figure out the best way to execute those wishes.

Meade was pleased. "[Grant] is so much more active than his predecessor, and agrees so well with me in his views,

I cannot but be rejoiced at his arrival, because I believe success to be the more probable," he later wrote to his wife. "My duty is plain, to continue quietly to discharge my duties, heartily co-operating with him and under him."

Grant and Meade launched their offensive against Lee by sending forward elements of the army across the Rapidan River on May 3, 1864. The rest of the army followed on May 4, crossing at Germanna Ford and Ely's Ford, using the two roads to prevent bottlenecking their large force. The maneuver also gave them flexibility. No one was quite sure how Lee might react—or even where, exactly, Lee was—so the parallel approaches across the river gave the army the option of several routes to get at the Confederates.

If Lee moved into his former position behind Mine Run, Grant intended to swing south of the creek and outflank his position. On the other hand, if Lee fell back toward Richmond, Grant would be in position to overtake the Confederates and force them to fight in open country, where he had little doubt his much larger army would prevail. No one in the Union high command seemed to seriously consider the possibility that Lee might attack them in the Wilderness.

When Lee did strike, then, on May 5, it sent part of the Federal command into near panic. What other tricks did the

Grant (pictured here with two members of his staff) had a reputation for keeping his cool during battle—a reputation he lived up to during the Battle of the Wilderness.

"I AM HEARTILY TIRED OF HEARING WHAT LEE IS GOING TO DO," GRANT FINALLY SNAPPED. "…GO BACK TO YOUR COMMAND, AND TRY TO THINK WHAT WE ARE GOING TO DO OURSELVES, INSTEAD OF WHAT LEE IS GOING TO DO."

—U. S. GRANT

Confederate commander have up his gold-braided sleeve, they fretted.

"I am heartily tired of hearing what Lee is going to do," Grant finally snapped. "Some of you always seem to think he is suddenly going to turn a double somersault, and land on our rear and on both our flanks at the same time. Go back to your command, and try to think what we are going to do ourselves, instead of what Lee is going to do."

Accurate information on that morning of May 5 proved hard to come by for Grant and Meade both. Union cavalry failed to properly scout out the Confederate position. Union corps commanders couldn't get a clear picture of the events unfolding right in front of them. The entire Federal army was strung out along the road for miles. And gray-clad troops poured and poured down one road, then another, filling the woods between.

The situation might have daunted a different man, but Grant, itching for a fight with Lee, issued a decisive command to Meade: "If any opportunity presents itself of pitching into a part of Lee's army, do so without giving time for disposition."

This, like Grant's approach to nearly everything else, represented a markedly different way of thinking for the Army of the Potomac. Lee always preferred to take the initiative, and former Federal commanders had always seemed to oblige him. Grant refused to let his army dance to Lee's tune any longer.

"No movement of the enemy seemed to puzzle or discon-cert him," said a correspondent. At one point, on the second day of battle, Confederate artillery fire swept close to Grant's headquarters. "General," said an officer, "wouldn't it be pru-dent to move headquarters…until the result of the present attack is known?" Grant puffed his cigar. "It strikes me," he replied, "that it would be better to order up some artillery and defend the present location."

It was classic Grant. After the first day at Shiloh, when the surprise Confederate attack had nearly driven Grant's army into the river, a near-despairing Sherman found his commander under a tree with a cigar. "Well, Grant," Sherman

The bulk of the Union army crossed into the Wilderness using Germanna Ford.

said, "we've had the devil's own day of it, haven't we?" "Yes," Grant replied. "Lick 'em tomorrow, though." And he did.

But despite his cool demeanor, Grant fully felt the weight of the responsibility he bore. On the evening of May 6, after the final threat of the day had been repulsed, after two days of unprecedented battlefield carnage, Grant gave up his whittling and his cigar smoking and retired to his tent. His chief of staff, Brigadier General John Rawlins, later said that he "had never before seen [Grant] show the slightest apprehension or sense of danger; but on that memorable night in the Wilderness it was much more than personal danger which confronted him. No one knew better than he that he was face to face with destiny, and there was no doubt that he realized it fully and understood perfectly that retreat from that field meant a great calamity to his country as well as to himself."

There in his tent, Rawlins said, face-down on his cot, Grant "gave vent to his feelings in a way which left no room to doubt that he was deeply moved."

The battle had whittled away his calm exterior at last.

But Grant's resolve remained. The general emerged from his tent a short time later to sit by the fire, stone faced, mulling his options.

He was ready to make another go at the Confederates, ready to try again to lick 'em tomorrow.

Ulysses S. Grant

"I have acted in every instance from a conscientious desire to do what was right, constitutional, within the law, and for the very best interests of the whole people." — Ulysses S. Grant

Ulysses S. Grant, during his postwar tenure as president of the United States.

Born on April 27, 1822, in Point Pleasant, Ohio, Hiram Ulysses Grant was the son of a tanner.

At age 17, Grant attended West Point, but a clerical error registered his name as "Ulysses S. Grant"—a name he decided to adopt since West Point refused to change it. Because the initials "U.S." also stood for "Uncle Sam," Grant's West Point friends started calling him "Sam" for short.

Grant graduated in 1843, twenty-first in his class of thirty-nine, and was assigned to serve in the Quartermaster's Department. When war broke out with Mexico, he served near the front lines, earning two battlefield promotions for bravery.

In August 1848, Grant married Julia Dent, and together they had four children. Grant's postwar service in the army took him to assignments far from his family, though, and he missed them terribly. He tried to counter the loneliness and boredom with drink. Charges of alcoholism dogged him for the rest of his career, although evidence suggests the charges were largely fabricated and, later, politically motivated.

Grant resigned his commission in 1854 and returned to his family's home in St. Louis, where he struggled to make ends meet. In 1860, he went to work in his father's leather shop, then located in Galena, Illinois.

The following year, when hostilities erupted between North and South, Grant earned a commission as a brigadier general of volunteers—a commission made possible largely through the intercession of a political sponsor. The appointment rescued Grant from obscurity.

In February 1862, he captured two key Confederate forts, Henry and Donelson, situated on the Tennessee and Cumberland Rivers. His capture of Donelson, in particular, made headlines because he offered no terms but "unconditional surrender"—

and thus the press nicknamed him "'Unconditional Surrender' Grant" to match his initials.

Grant scored key victories at Shiloh in April of that year, at Vicksburg in July 1863, and in Chattanooga in November 1863. The following March, President Lincoln named Grant commander in chief of all Union armies. While he coordinated all Union movements, Grant traveled with the Army of the Potomac, eventually forcing the surrender of Robert E. Lee at Appomattox on April 9, 1865.

Following the war, Grant ran for the White House as a Republican. He was elected the eighteenth president, serving two terms, from 1869-1877. Charged with overseeing the implementation of Reconstruction, Grant discovered that Northerners had little interest in or patience with the violence that gripped the South, and although he did much to preserve the rights of freedmen, it was ultimately a losing battle. Grant's administration was also notorious for scandal, although Grant himself had no personal hand in any of it.

In 1880, supporters persuaded Grant to come out of retirement and run for a third term, but he could not gain a majority of votes to earn his party's nomination. Following that, he retired to a quiet life with his wife in a New York City townhouse.

In 1884, one of Grant's financial partners swindled him, leaving the former president bankrupt. To repay his debts, he agreed to write his memoirs—a project overseen by his friend, Mark Twain. At about the same time, Grant was diagnosed with terminal throat cancer caused by his years of cigar smoking. He finished his memoirs just days before his death. Today, the memoirs still stand as one of the great works of American nonfiction. Grant died on July 23, 1885. He and his wife are buried in New York City's Riverside Park.

Grant and his favorite horse, Cincinnatus.

The Two Generals

Major General
George Gordon Meade
and Lieutenant General
Ulysses S. Grant.

As he marched into the Wilderness, George F. Williams of the 146th New York infantry recalled seeing the Union army's commanders standing in a nook in the woods along the roadside:

General Meade was standing on the bank that overlooked the road, his soldierly figure contrasting strangely with that of the lieutenant-general, who was seated on a decaying stump, apparently more interested in the toe of his boot than our movements. An unlighted cigar was between Grant's teeth, and he chewed his weed viciously. When our regiment came in front of the two generals, I caught a glimpse of General Grant's eyes, as he lifted them for a moment. Clear and steady, calm and confident, this great leader seemed in that single glance to take in the face of every man within his range; and I was impressed by the strong will betokened by the square chin and the firm mouth of the man who was planning and conducting our campaign. The tall, courtly figure of Meade, his trim gray hair, and neat regulation cap, gave him a martial look, as he leaned on his saber; while the heavy frame of Grant, who wore no sword, seemed the very opposite of my preconceived ideas of our new commander. The wide-brimmed hat, pulled down over his eyes, and the closely clipped beard, made the renowned chieftain appear so unlike a soldier that it needed the uniform and the broad shoulder-strap, with its row of triple stars, to remind one that here was a warrior already famous.

CHAPTER FOUR

LEE MOVES INTO
THE WILDERNESS

General Robert E. Lee, commander of the Confederate Army of Northern Virginia.

All spring long, Robert E. Lee watched and worried.

Much of his success as the commander of the Army of Northern Virginia had stemmed from his ability to take the measure of his opponent. It had allowed him to act with audacity, as when he turned, with his back to the Potomac, to challenge George McClellan at Antietam in September 1862, or when he divided his army not once but twice in front of a cowed "Fighting Joe" Hooker at Chancellorsville in May 1863.

Now, in the spring of 1864, he faced a new Federal opponent: Lieutenant General Ulysses S. Grant. While Lee didn't seem overly impressed at the news of Grant's appointment, he wasn't immediately sure what to make of Grant, either.

But Lee's trusted "Old Warhorse," Lieutenant General James Longstreet, knew exactly what to make of the new Union commander. "That man will fight us every day and every hour till the end of the war," warned Longstreet, who knew Grant's temperament if anyone did: He and Grant had been friends in the pre-war army, and Longstreet had served as best man at Grant's wedding.

"It behooves us to be on the alert, or we will be deceived," Lee worried. "You know that is part of Grant's tactics." Lee even worried that press reports about Grant's plans had "an appearance of design…intended to mislead us as to the enemy's intention."

During the early spring of 1864, Lee worried about reports of a Union build-up of men and material.

Every piece of intelligence that came to Lee during March and April gave him more to worry about. "[A] large number of recruits are being sent to the Army of the Potomac," said one informant, who "expressed surprize at the number of troops conveyed on the [railroad]." Every train, Lee told Confederate President Jefferson Davis, brings the Army of the Potomac new recruits. "Their clothes are too new & overcoats of too deep a blue for old troops," he reported to Richmond.

As he worried about the swelling numbers of the Federal army, Lee also worried about the uncertain number of men in his own army. Many had deserted over the winter because of a lack of supplies or because of their own proximity to home, although as the spring campaign season neared, many of the stragglers began to return to the ranks.

He had also detached a significant portion of his army— some 11,000 men under Longstreet—to special duty in Tennessee. Throughout March and into April, Lee prodded Longstreet to keep an eye on his front, and as soon as Longstreet felt comfortable that the Federals there had withdrawn, he was to return to Virginia as quickly as possible.

Lee was also concerned enough about manpower to issue a circular to his men: "I hope that few of the soldiers of this army will find it necessary at any time in the coming campaign to surrender themselves prisoners of war. We cannot spare brave men to fill Federal prisons."

Even as he worried about having enough men, he worried about how to feed and clothe them. "The great obstacle everywhere is scarcity of supplies," Lee told Longstreet. Conditions were tight enough that Lee's wife sent him weekly caches of socks to distribute to soldiers.

Still, conditions weren't as bad as they'd been the previous winter, noted Lee's chief of staff, Colonel Walter Taylor. "Our army is in excellent condition in every way," he wrote. "Its morale is not to be surpassed—its sanitary condition was never so good—it is now well fed—and strange to relate is well and entirely shod. More could not be said in favor of any army that ever took the field."

By the time the campaign opened, Lee had some 66,000 men available to him, including Longstreet's corps. Overall, the army was slightly larger than it had been when he'd achieved his great victory at Chancellorsville the previous May. After that, as Lee moved north into Pennsylvania, the army's size swelled to 75,000—although Confederates took heavy casualties at the Battle of Gettysburg in early July. No one considered Gettysburg as anything other than a setback, though, and certainly no one looked at it as the "High Water Mark of the Confederacy" (a convenient conceit crafted by a marketing-savvy man named John Badger Bachelder who, in the 1890s, worked to promote Gettysburg as a tourism destination).

At the start of the Gettysburg Campaign in early June, Lee spent a night at Ellwood. Perhaps there, in the yard outside the house where his own father had written his memoirs, Lee reflected on his own fortunes of war. Certainly, by the time he wrote to his wife when he reached Culpeper a few days later, he was in a ruminating mood. "The country here looks very green & pretty notwithstanding the ravages of war," Lee wrote. "[Y]ou must remember me in your prayers, & implore the Lord of Hosts for the removal of the terrible scourge with which He has thought best to afflict our bleeding country."

"[Y]OU MUST REMEMBER ME IN YOUR PRAYERS, & IMPLORE THE LORD OF HOSTS FOR THE REMOVAL OF THE TERRIBLE SCOURGE WITH WHICH HE HAS THOUGHT BEST TO AFFLICT OUR BLEEDING COUNTRY."

—ROBERT E. LEE

Confederate Lieutenant General James Longstreet, Lee's "Old Warhorse."

As summer stretched into fall, the morale of the army—and the Confederacy in general—remained high. "The Army of Northern Virginia alone, as the last hope of the South… will sooner or later by its own unaided power win the independence of the Confederacy," wrote a Georgia officer with unbridled confidence.

Throughout the fall Lee, too, remained confident—if somewhat frustrated—as the armies tussled in a series of minor engagements and skirmishes. Although neither side scored any decisive victories, Lee successfully demonstrated his continued ability to parry movements by the much larger Federal army. The final confrontation of the campaign occurred along Mine Run, just seven miles west of the Wilderness, in the last days of November. The Union commander, Major General George Gordon Meade, called off a planned assault at the last moment after getting a closer look at the strength of the Confederate fortifications.

Meade withdrew his army north of the Rapidan River, toward its supply bases around Culpeper Court House and Brandy Station, to spend the winter. Lee remained south of the river, spreading his army between Mine Run and Orange Court House. He knew spring would bring a renewed Federal offensive, and he watched from afar all winter long as the Federals prepared. Grant's appointment and subsequent decision to campaign with the Army of the Potomac added one more unknown element to the mix.

When Longstreet returned in mid-April, Lee held him in reserve near the rail junction of Gordonsville. That way, depending on the direction Grant eventually advanced, Lee could send Longstreet on one of several routes to help counter the Federal thrust. Ever aggressive and ever looking to grasp the initiative, Lee waited impatiently for Grant to make that first move, but he had no other choice. In the meantime, he prepared his army so it could respond when the time came. "If I am forced to retire from this line, either by a flank movement of the enemy or the want of supplies," Lee warned Davis, "great injury will befall us."

When the Union army moved into the Wilderness, it presented a target too tempting for Lee to pass up. The Northern army made itself even more vulnerable by bivouacking in the Wilderness on the night of May 4 instead of marching through as quickly as possible.

The troops could sense the building tension. "Everything indicates preparation for active service about the 1st of May," a Confederate surgeon wrote. "Genl. Grant's wings have to be clipped, and I think Genl. Lee can do him that honor."

Even Lee showed renewed vigor at the thought of battle. Taylor noted that "it really seemed to do him good to look forward to the trial of strength soon to ensue between himself and the present idol of the North."

Grant showed his hand on May 3 when advance elements of his army began to cross the Rapidan River, with the bulk of the army following on May 4. "[W]hether with the intention of attacking, or moving towards Fredericksburg, I am not able to say," Lee wrote to Davis. "But it is apparent that the long threatened effort to take Richmond has begun, and that the enemy has collected all his available force to accomplish it."

Lee had watched and worried long enough.

Rather than let the Federal movement play out further, Lee chose to seize the initiative. He pushed his army forward along two parallel roads, the Orange Turnpike and, just to its south, the Orange Plank Road, in the hope of catching the Federals on the march and off guard. The impenetrable Wilderness would make it difficult for Grant to respond effectively despite his superior numbers.

"The troops are all in excellent spirits, and eager for the fray," said a South Carolinian. "Gen. Grant's glory will soon vanish away, and his great name buried along with those of his unfortunate predecessors."

Robert E. Lee

"Duty is the sublimest word in the language. You can never do more than your duty. You should never wish to do less."
— Robert E. Lee

Robert E. Lee, during his postwar tenure as president of Washington College.

Robert E. Lee was born on January 19, 1807, at Stratford Hall, Virginia, into one of the state's most prominent families. His mother, Anne Carter Lee, was the daughter of the state's richest man; his father, Henry "Light Horse Harry" Lee, was a Revolutionary War hero and friend of George Washington. Unfortunately, the elder Lee was also a poor financial manager, and he died, disgraced and debt-ridden, when his son Robert was only eleven.

In the summer of 1825, Lee went to West Point. He graduated second in the Class of 1829 and, in his four years, never earned a demerit for misconduct. After graduation, Lee worked as an army engineer, traveling the country to build and strengthen various fortifications.

In 1831, Lee married Mary Anna Randolph Custis, great-granddaughter of Martha Washington. They had seven children.

When war broke out with Mexico in 1846, Lee served on the staff of General-in-Chief Winfield Scott, distinguishing himself by earning three battlefield promotions for bravery. Scott praised him as "the very best soldier I ever saw in the field."

In 1852, Lee began a term as superintendent at West Point. Three years later, he was transferred to Texas where, for the first time, he exercised command over troops in the field.

In 1859, while home in Arlington, Virginia, Lee received emergency orders to quell an uprising at the Federal arsenal at Harpers Ferry, Virginia. With cavalry captain James Ewell Brown "Jeb" Stuart at his side, Lee traveled with a company of Marines to the arsenal. There, he found abolitionist John Brown and his men locked in a firehouse with hostages. On Lee's order, the Marines stormed the firehouse, capturing Brown.

When Southern states began to secede from the Union in 1861, the Lincoln administration offered Lee command of the entire Union army to quell the rebellion. Unable to fight against Virginia, which he called his "home country," Lee turned down Lincoln's offer and resigned his commission.

The first year of the war was rough on Lee. After organizing Virginia's defenses, he commanded troops in the Allegheny Mountains, but suffered several setbacks. He then served as chief military adviser to Confederate President Jefferson Davis, a desk job that ill-suited a man who wished to be in the field.

Lee with his favorite horse, Traveller.

Lee got his chance on May 31, 1862, when the commander of the Confederate army outside Richmond, General Joseph Johnston, was wounded in battle. Davis asked Lee to take over. As his first order of business, Lee strengthened the fortifications around the capital to free up men to fight. It soon pitched into the Federal army in a series of battles known as the Seven Days, driving the Federals away from the gates of Richmond.

Rechristening his force the Army of Northern Virginia, Lee led his men on an unprecedented string of battlefield victories. "Providence raises up the man for the time," a Richmond newspaper once said of him, "and a man for this occasion, we believe, has been raised up in Robert E. Lee, the Washington of the second American Revolution."

But it was not to be. By the spring of 1865, the Army of Northern Virginia was worn down by battle, attrition, desertion, and deprivation. Lee surrendered at Appomattox on April 9, then returned to Richmond for a few quiet months.

In August, Washington College in Lexington, Virginia, offered Lee its presidency. He accepted the position and served there until his death on October 12, 1870. After his death, Trustees voted to change the school's name to Washington and Lee. There, beneath the college chapel, Lee and his wife and family lie buried.

On August 5, 1975, President Gerald Ford formally pardoned Lee. Lee had filed an oath of allegiance with President Andrew Johnson's administration, but a clerk lost the certificate before it was officially filed. In issuing the pardon, Ford said, "General Lee's character has been an example to succeeding generations, making the restoration of his citizenship an event in which every American can take pride."

CHAPTER FIVE

QUANDARY AT SAUNDERS FIELD

———

Today, a monument in Saunders Field marks the location where New York Zouaves made a desperate charge against the Confederate position.

There was "something oppressive in the dim light and the strange quiet," a Union officer noted. He could not tell why, or where his feeling came from.

It was May 5, an hour after daybreak.

The Union army had already begun its march for the day, and although the narrow, forest-choked roads made movement difficult, everything seemed to be going relatively well. Major General Gouverneur Warren's Fifth Corps led the march. A few miles behind him, near Germanna Ford, Major General John Sedgwick's Sixth Corps followed. To the east, along Ely's Ford Road, Major Winfield Scott Hancock's Second Corps traveled a parallel route. Still on the north side of the Rapidan River, Major General Ambrose E. Burnside's Ninth Corps brought up the rear.

The wings of the army would move a little farther south, then swing westward to search out the Army of Northern Virginia and do battle. Somewhere out there they knew, miles beyond the Wilderness, the Confederates waited.

Nearly all of Warren's corps had passed beyond the Orange Turnpike, following a wagon road that skirted the Ellwood plantation and led to Parker's Store along the Orange Plank Road a few miles to the south. The rear guard, under Brigadier General Charles Griffin, prepared to pack up and join the rest of their corps, but then one of the pickets spotted something, like an early-morning mirage, far down the road just before it dissolved into the horizon: horsemen in

Confederate Lieutenant General Richard Ewell.

Union Major General Gouverneur Warren.

gray. The pickets watched as the horsemen drew closer—with gray-clad infantry marching behind them. "With the aide of my glass," wrote a Federal colonel, "I could plainly see the enemy filing off to the right and left of the road and apparently massing his forces."

The Confederates belonged to Lieutenant General Richard Ewell's Second Corps. Lee had sent them as the first wave in an attempt to delay the Federal movement while the rest of the Confederate army got into position. As Ewell's men filed from the road into the forest, they began to dig trenches at the crest of a ridge that ran along the western edge of a clearing known as Saunders Field.

"I do not believe that Warren ever had a greater surprise in his life," wrote a staff officer who saw the Fifth Corps commander's reaction when a courier arrived with the news. Lee was supposed to be miles away, yet reports now flooded in that indicated an unknown number of Confederates threatened the Federal column.

Warren halted his march immediately. He set up headquarters at Ellwood, which provided him with as good of a view of the tangled Wilderness as he was liable to get, then ordered his men to deploy. He also sent word to Meade who, in turn, forwarded the news to Grant. "If any opportunity presents itself of pitching into a part of Lee's army," Grant replied, "do so without giving time for disposition." To do so, Warren had to shift his men from marching formation into line of battle—and he had to do so in the indomitable thickness of the Wilderness. "Just imagine the difficulty a single unencumbered man would have getting through those thickets," said a Pennsylvanian, "and then think what a task it was to take a line of battle through those woods; the men encumbered as ours were with knap sacks on backs, three days rations in haversack, gun in hand and 60 rounds of ammunition."

Some of Warren's men began to dig earthworks of their own. At the far right of the line, where the rear guard had been, Warren ordered Griffin to send a force forward to probe the enemy. Griffin balked because his flanks would be unprotected. Sedgwick's eventual arrival to the north of Warren helped,

but the Federal position was still highly vulnerable. Struggling against the Wilderness, Warren couldn't get men in line quickly enough.

By 10:30, word arrived that a large Confederate force had appeared on the Orange Plank Road to the south. Lee had apparently sent not one but two spearheads toward the Union column.

Grant managed to stem that crisis by noon, but along the Turnpike, Warren had still not launched an attack. Meade, under pressure from Grant for all-out action, tore into Warren, who in turn tore into Griffin, who continued to demur. When Griffin finally did advance sometime around 12:30, it was against his own better judgment. At least some of his men felt differently, though. "The officers and men all along the line were eager and enthusiastic, and evidently anticipated, without thought of dread, the first fight of the campaign," said one officer.

By one o'clock, Griffin's men reached the eastern edge of Saunders Field. One of the largest open areas in the Wilderness, the unevenly shaped field measured some 400 yards long by 800 yards wide. The Turnpike ran directly down the

The long open hilltop around Ellwood, here seen from the Wilderness Tavern, provided one of the only useful artillery platforms in the Wilderness.

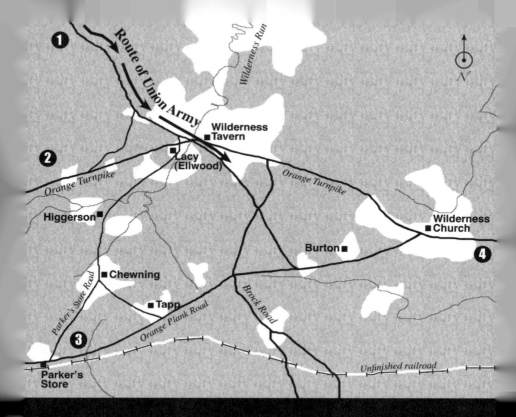

On May 4, the Union Army's Fifth and Sixth Corps entered the Wilderness from the direction of Germanna Ford (1) while the Second Corps crossed at Ely's Ford farther east. Army commander Major General George Gordon Meade ordered a halt overnight so the wagon trains could catch up. Shortly after first light on May 5, Confederate Lieutenant General Richard Ewell led his Second Corps onto the field along the Orange Turnpike and dug in along the western edge of Saunders Field (2), inviting the Union Fifth Corps to attack. Midmorning, Confederate Major General A. P. Hill led his Third Corps onto the field along the Orange Plank Road (3). Union cavalry, intercepting the Confederates near Parker's Store, barely slowed Hill's advance. Elements of the Sixth Corps intercepted Hill long enough for the Union Second Corps arrive from the direction of Chancellorsville (4).

middle of the field, and a swale bisected it from southeast to northwest. "The last crop of the old field had been corn," said one soldier, "and among its stubble that day were sown the seeds of glory."

On the north side of the turnpike, Federals marched into the clearing, protected somewhat by the ravine as they moved downhill. But as they ascended the far side, Confederates opened fire on them. A large body of Confederates also appeared on Griffin's unprotected right flank. "Men disappeared as if the earth had swallowed them," said one New Yorker making the assault. "It seemed as if the regiment had been annihilated."

More Federals charged into the fight, but to no avail. An infantryman remembered being "exposed to a terrific cross fire, which mowed down men by scores. No troops could stand this and our left broke and ran. This of course made bad worse and the entire line broke."

Grant, back near Germanna Ford when fighting broke out, quickly scribbled a note to Meade: "If any opportunity presents itself of pitching into a part of Lee's army, do so without giving time for disposition."

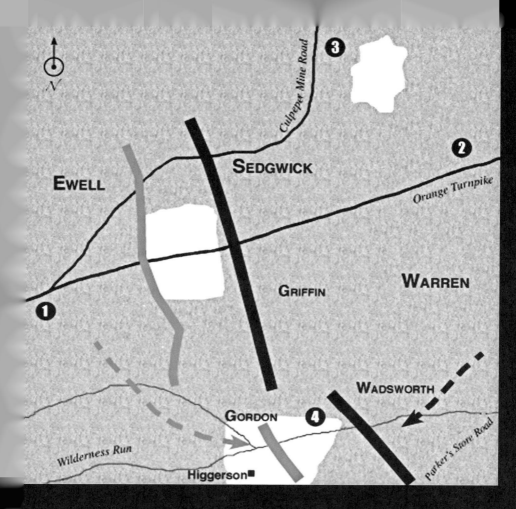

On the morning of May 5, 1864, Confederate Second Corps commander Lieutenant General Richard Ewell approached along the Orange Turnpike (1) and directed his men into position along the western edge of Saunders Field. Union Fifth Corps commander Major General Gouverneur Warren, after much delay, ordered his men to attack down the turnpike (2). Later, Sixth Corps commander Major General John Sedgwick, farther back in the line or march, sent men down the Culpeper Mine Road (3) to link up with Warren. As the afternoon wore on, fighting shifted southward toward the Higgerson farm (4), where men commanded by Brigadier General James Wadsworth of Warren's Fifth Corps clashed with elements of Ewell's Second Corps commanded by Brigadier General John B. Gordon.

The 140th New York, a Zouave regiment decked out in bright red pants, blue vests, and turbans, managed to crest the far ridge. The Confederate brigadier there, General George "Maryland" Steuart, failed to take best advantage of the terrain when he had ordered his men to entrench. His line sat behind the crest of the ridge, rather than in front of it, denying his men the opportunity to fire at Federals crossing the open field. For a few moments, the Federals managed to swarm into the Confederate line before numbers turned against them. Adding to the chaos, a pair of Union guns wheeled into the middle of Saunders Field began to fire rounds into the Confederate works right where the New Yorkers were fighting. Casualties among the artillery crews would eventually end the shelling, and the two cannon would fall into Confederate hands.

Meanwhile, from the northwest edge of the field, where the Union line had broken, more Confederates swept in behind the New Yorkers, surrounding them. Another Zouave regiment also found itself trapped. Together, survivors from the two units ran the gauntlet in retreat, "creating a fantastic spectacle as the wearers ran to and fro over the field, firing and shouting."

South of the Turnpike, the Federals fared a little better. The brigade of General Joseph Bartlett broke through the Confederate line and routed the men of Brigadier General John M. Jones. Jones, trying to rally his men and vowing to die before giving another inch, was shot dead from his horse. Confusion caused even more Confederates to withdraw. Soon, recalled a Pennsylvania officer, "[o]n we went, o'er briar, o'er brake, o'er logs and o'er bogs through the underbrush and overhanging limbs, for about three quarters of a mile, yelling like so many demons."

Confederates took a position along the crest of a hill that afforded them a clear view of Saunders Field.

As the Federals prepared to launch their attack across Saunders Field, the Confederates strengthened their position and waited. "All nature seems to expect some awful shock," one of them said.

A pair of Union Zouave regiments found themselves isolated after one of them, the 140th New York, broke through the Confederate line.

Bartlett's men soon found themselves isolated, though, and they began to take fire on their flanks. They turned about and made their way back to Saunders Field, first in good order then pell-mell. Many barely avoided being captured.

By 2:30 p.m., the assaults along the Orange Turnpike were over. Meade tried to renew action less than an hour later, sending Sedgwick's corps against the Confederate position, but poor organization and the thick Wilderness itself prevented success. For the rest of the day, most of the significant fighting across the battlefield shifted to the south.

"All nature seems to expect some awful shock," said a member of the Stonewall Brigade as he had waited for the day's action to begin.

The fighting in Saunders Field on May 5 proved shocking enough, indeed—but the real shock, the one nobody yet knew, was that the fighting between the two armies that had started in this field would continue unabated all summer long.

The Positions of the Armies

A reporter from the *Boston Journal*, traveling with the Army of the Potomac, offered readers a look at the positions of each army as they prepared to square off:

Years ago a turnpike was built from Fredericksburg to Orange Court House; but in the days when there was a mania for plank roads another corporation constructed a plank road between the same places.... General Grant has established his head-quarters at [a] crossing, his flag waving from a knoll west of the road. A mile and a half out on the turnpike, on a ridge...and there...I can see long lines of rebel infantry—the sunlight beaming from the bayonet and gun barrel.

Before the contest begins, go with me up to the old Wilderness tavern, which stands on the...plank road, and take a view of a portion of the battle field. It will be a limited view, for there are few open spaces in the Wilderness.

From the old tavern you look west. At your feet is a brook, flowing from the southwest, and another smaller stream from the northwest, joining their waters at the crossing of the turn-pike and the plank road. The turnpike rises over a ridge between the two streams. On the south slope is the house of Major Lacy, owner of a house at Falmouth [Chatham], used by our forces after the battle of Fredericksburg. It is a beautiful view. A smooth lawn in front of the house, meadows green with the verdure of spring; beyond the meadows are hills thickly wooded, tall oaks and pine and cedar thickets. On the right hand side of the turnpike the ridge is more broken, and also thickly set with small trees and bushes. A mile and a half out from the crossing of the two roads the ridge breaks down into a ravine. Gen Lee has possession of the western bank, Grant the eastern. It is such a mixture of woods, underbrush, thickets, ravines, hills, hollows, knolls, that one is bewildered in passing through it, and to describe it a complete bewilderment to writer and reader.

Ellwood stood as one of the few open spaces in the untamed Wilderness.

Topography of the Wilderness

A map, even one marked with elevation lines, presents only a two-dimensional view of a battlefield. However, the three-dimensional features of the landscape frequently dictate the events and outcomes of battle. Saunders Field provides some useful illustrations because the cleared space gives modern visitors a look at the undulating terrain that's elsewhere obscured by trees.

The undulations of the ground frequently served to funnel advancing soldiers in odd directions, causing misdirection and delay. When covered with thick undergrowth, as they were throughout the Wilderness, such topographical features made straight and clear navigation nearly impossible.

A swale cuts across Saunders Field, from southeast to northwest. As soldiers marched down into the swale, the uphill slope shielded them from enemy fire. When the 140th New York crossed the field, for instance, the first volley from Confederates went well over their heads. But because of the diagonal cut of the swale, Federals advancing up the slope south of the road found themselves vulnerable to fire from the very same Confederates who couldn't shoot at the advancing New Yorkers.

The Orange Turnpike cut through the middle of the undulating ground of Saunders Field. The field's topography dictated much of the fighting there on May 5.

Likewise, artillerists who set up pieces near the bottom of the swale couldn't see their targets over the crest of the hill. Eventually, they turned their cannons to face northwest, up the length of the swale, where they could see Confederates emerging from the woods on the Union flank.

The bottom of the swale gets marshy during rainy spells. Dozens of other such low-lying areas across the Wilderness created unexpected wet spots that impeded movement—and in the heavy foliage, such wet spots proved almost impossible to detect in advance.

The Orange Turnpike, which brought both armies to the battlefield, still bisects the field today as modern Route 20. In Saunders Field, it's easy to envision how a column of troops marching down the road could file off to one side of the road or the other and, taking advantage of the open space, quickly spread out into line of battle. That also makes it easy to envision why Lee wanted to avoid giving the Federal army any opportunity to do that.

By walking across the field, a visitor will see how dramatically the view changes from spot to spot, how perspectives shift, how the land unfolds. Unseen dips and rises will reveal themselves.

It's all visible in Saunders Field—one of the few places in the Wilderness where anything was visible at all.

From the air, the undulations of Saunders Field look more apparent, but from the ground, the field's contours are deceptive. The Orange Turnpike, now modern Route 20, still runs through the center of the field.

CHAPTER SIX

HOMEPLACES IN THE SWIRL OF WAR

The Chewning house, known also as "Mount View."

The Chewning farm sat atop a long, open plateau that rose like an island out of the forest. From the high ground, visitors could see Virginia's Blue Ridge far to the west. Closer, just a few miles to the northeast of the two-and-a-half story farmhouse, visitors could see the Wilderness Tavern. For entertainment, family members living in the farmhouse would sometimes use field glasses to watch pigeons strut about on the tavern roof.

To the southwest, visitors could plainly see Parker's Store a mile away. A sun-dappled country lane ran down to the abandoned store from the hilltop.

The farm, christened "Mount View" by its owners, William and Permelia Chewning, had sprung up on the plateau sometime before 1836. Compared to their neighbors at the Ellwood plantation, the Chewnings owned a small farm: some one hundred and fifty acres, including the eighty acres of cleared land along the top of the plateau, where they grew wheat, rye, oats, corn, and tobacco. Thirteen slaves worked the land and lived in cabins that sat to the east of the farm's big barn.

The Chewnings had ten children, spaced so far apart that the eldest had married and moved away before the youngest were even born. By 1860, on the eve of the war, only the youngest two remained at home, 34-year-old Jane and 26-year-old Absalom. William and Absalom worked the farm side by side. Father also taught son the family tradition of shoemaking.

The Higgerson house.

The Union army, on the verge of a complete breakthrough, found themselves facing a line of Confederate artillery posted at the Widow Tapp farm.

One of the family's other daughters lived less than a mile away. Also named Permelia, she had married Benjamin Higgerson, a farmer, and together they raised four children. They had a tobacco barn near the house as well as a family cemetery.

The Chewnings and Higgersons mostly avoided the war, and the war avoided them. Only Absalom served any time in the Confederate army—a seven-day stint cut short for health reasons. After that, the government assigned him a job at Catharine Furnace, as a blacksmith, where they called him "Boss Smith."

When the war did arrive, though, it first did so in quiet, tragic fashion. In the late fall of 1862, Permelia Higgerson took into her home a wounded Confederate. Too late, the family discovered he had smallpox. Benjamin contracted the disease and, on Christmas Day, he died. Permelia buried him in the family cemetery near the house.

William Chewning died the following June as the result of an accident at a local grist mill. By that point, most of the Chewning's slaves had deserted the family. Only Thomas, a 50-year-old slave who served as Absalom's personal attendant, remained.

Federal soldiers moved through the area in the fall of 1863 and again in the spring of 1864. Like many of her neighbors, Permelia Chewning placed her silverware in boxes and buried them in her garden for safekeeping. When Northern soldiers finally did pay her a visit in early May, Permelia was home alone. By afternoon, the soldiers—elements of General

**Permelia Higgerson
and her son Edgar.**

Samuel Crawford's brigade—had butchered the pigs from the farm's hog pen and, after bullying Permelia out of her home, set to roasting pork in the big kitchen fireplace. One of Permelia's cousins, riding in on horseback that evening, tricked the Federals into surrendering even as Permelia made her way through the darkening Wilderness to the safety of a neighbor's house. It was well she fled, for early the next morning sharp fighting broke out in the fields around her hilltop house.

May 5 turned out to be far more eventful for Permelia's daughter down at the Higgerson farm. Federal troops swept across her property in the early afternoon, much to her chagrin. A Pennsylvanian heard the younger Permelia express "her views on the matter in strong language," calling the Federals "a pack of cowardly Yankees." After Confederates repulsed the Union advance, the jubilant woman taunted and derided the Federals as they retreated.

Other local families had encounters of their own with Federal soldiers. A detachment of New Yorkers, trying to find the rest of their regiment, sought out the "lord of the manor" at an unidentified farmhouse, probably belonging to the Webb family, to serve as a guide. "Couldn't think of it," the farmer replied. "When I'm gone, who knows who might tote off my wife and young uns. Couldn't think of it, sir."
"No excuses will do, sir," the Federal captain replied. The farmer's daughter then intervened. "Oh, sir!" she said, "you

On the afternoon of May 5, Generals Grant and Meade (both on horseback in the center) paid a visit to Ellwood to consult with Major General Gouverneur Warren (standing left).

would not think of taking my father? What should we do were some accident to befall him?" The captain promised no harm would come to the father, so the daughter asked to go along, too.

Another young girl, four-year-old Eliza Tapp, lived with her widowed mother and grandmother in a cabin to the southeast of Mount View near the Orange Plank Road. The mother, Catherine Tapp, rented the forty-acre farmstead from J. Horace Lacy, the owner of Ellwood. Plum and cherry trees surrounded the Tapp home, which also had a corncrib, a stable, and another outbuilding. Eliza heard the sounds of cannon and mistook it for thunder. A great storm was brewing, she thought. Not long after, she and her family fled westward down the Orange Plank Road, and she remembered the patter of large raindrops on the road around her. Only later did she learn that the raindrops were Minié balls.

Any farmer's field, any open space around a family farmhouse, attracted the armies as they grappled against each other in the bramble-choked forest. Fighting swirled into those open spaces, displacing the people who lived there or forcing them into hiding.

The Chewnings' farm attracted particular attention because of the view it offered of the surrounding countryside. In the late afternoon of May 7, Robert E. Lee met with his subordinate A. P. Hill on the front porch of the house, and there they observed that the Union army was in motion.

Later that week, when Absalom returned to the house from the furnace, traveling along a narrow path through the dark woods, he stumbled over bodies strewn across the pathway. His house, he discovered, was deserted. He eventually found his mother, and with his former slave, Thorton, the three returned to Mount View.

"They did have a home to come back to, even if it was in an awful mess," recalled Absalom's granddaughter, many years later, passing along family lore; "the floors in the big front room were very blood stained, and blood would not wash out of the wooden floor boards, so they had to be taken up and replaced. The fences were torn down as well as some of the

In the wake of the fighting that swirled across local farms, slave cabins like these were frequently turned into field hospitals for wounded soldiers.

Today, a country lane leads up to the site of the old Chewning farm.

smaller servants cabins. Yes the house was still there—as well as the barn and Absalom's workshop, but they were all riddled with bullets and everything inside was a terrible mess, all broken and torn." Even the silverware buried in the vegetable garden was missing.

Like so many of their neighbors, the Chewnings returned after the battle and did the only thing they could: They tried to rebuild their lives in the hardscrabble Wilderness.

Ellwood in the Swirl

By the evening of May 5, small groups of orderlies, clerks, teamsters, and cooks milled about on the grounds around Ellwood. They sat, in groups of twos and threes, around camp-fires. Some, using their jackets as pillows, had lain down to sleep despite the clatter of cooking pots and the braying of donkeys and horses from the nearby wagons. Nearby, a line of artillery stood silent—a sharp contrast to the thunder they had bellowed all day.

Inside, in the large, high-ceilinged parlor to the left of the front door, lit by the flickering light of several candles and a globe lantern, Major General Gouverneur K. Warren sat at a table and looked at numbers. "[H]is long, coal-black hair was streaming away from his finely expressive forehead, the only feature rising unclouded above the habitual gloom of his duskily sallow face," remembered one of his staff officers.

Warren had chosen Ellwood as his headquarters that morning. The open hills around the house provided a perfect platform for artillery—especially important because of a lack of good artillery positions closer to the front. Ellwood also offered Warren easy routes of communication to portions of his corps down both the Orange Turnpike and Parker's Store Road.

At 2:30 that afternoon, Grant and Meade paid Warren a visit. Even from the high, clear ground of Ellwood, which

A sketch of the open fields around Ellwood, as seen from Wilderness Run.

afforded a good view, it took the generals nearly half an hour to get oriented to the battleground because the Wilderness presented such a confusing landscape.

By then, wounded from the battle along the Turnpike had begun streaming back from the front. Surgeons had erected field hospitals near the northern border of the Lacy property, around the Wilderness Tavern, and they set about their own bloody work.

It was with his chief surgeon and his chief of staff that Warren met now as they pored over the numbers of killed and wounded during the first day of battle. "It will never do, to make a showing of such heavy losses," Warren finally said. The numbers, he suggested, would have to be softened.

The Army of the Potomac departed from the Wilderness with the true scope of horror downplayed, yet the dead and wounded left an everlasting mark on Ellwood. The twenty-six graves that had been dug within a few hundred yards of the house hardly even began to tell the full story. "Many graves were ploughed over by the tenant, before I returned to the County," wrote J. Horace Lacy in 1866. "Therefore other graves [are] unmarked which I could not designate, though the places are known."

After the Battle of Chancellorsville, when the house had been used as a hospital, blood had stained its hardwood floors. After the Battle of the Wilderness, blood had drenched Ellwood's very soil.

As the two armies collided in the Wilderness, Ellwood became a central hub of activity for the Army of the Potomac.

CHAPTER SEVEN
THE SPRAWL OF BATTLE

Ellwood served as the headquarters for the Union Fifth Corps.

Union Brigadier General James S. Wadsworth.

Two roads, roughly parallel, stabbed into the right flank of the Union column as it marched south on May 5. The northern road, the Orange Turnpike, shot straight; the southern, the Orange Plank Road, took a less direct route.

Lieutenant General Richard Ewell's column of Confederates, marching along the northern road, thus reached the Union position sooner than Lieutenant General A. P. Hill's column, marching along the less-direct southern road.

And so, fighting in the Wilderness started along the Turnpike and shifted south as the day progressed.

When Griffin sent his Federals sweeping across Saunders Field at 1:00 p.m., Brigadier General James Wadsworth advanced his men to the south, protecting Griffin's left flank. Whereas Griffin's men moved through one of the largest open spaces in the Wilderness, Wadsworth had the Wilderness itself to push through. His advance quickly stalled.

Colonel Roy Stone, at the center of Wadsworth's formation, had particular difficulty. His brigade advanced along the southern edge of Wilderness Run, a swampy depression one Pennsylvanian described as the "champion mud hole of mud holes." On either side of Stone's men, the rest of Wadsworth's division moved forward, crossing a clearing known as Spring Hill, the site of the Higgerson farm. With Stone's men literally bogged down, a large gap developed in Wadsworth's line.

While Federal forces to the north of him advanced across the open space of Saunders Field, James Wadsworth's men had to advance through the thick Wilderness, which quickly led to trouble.

And into that gap poured the Confederates of Brigadier General John B. Gordon, freshly arrived on the field from the Orange Turnpike.

With things by now going badly for Confederates along the south end of Saunders Field, Gordon had been directed into line to bolster the Confederate position. What he found was an infantry commander's dream: to the north and south of him, he saw the unprotected flanks of lines of Union soldiers.

"Looking down that line from Grant's right toward his left, there first would have been seen a long stretch of blue uniforms, then a short stretch of gray, then another still longer of blue, in one continuous line...." Gordon later wrote with much enthusiasm in his hyperbolic memoir. "In such a crisis, when moments count for hours, when the fate of a command hangs upon instantaneous decision, the responsibility of the commander is almost overwhelming; but the very extremity of the danger electrifies his brain to abnormal activity."

Instead of crossing the field, where he would've encountered Stone's men in the bog, Gordon swung some of his men

northward and some southward, where they pitched into "the astounded Federals, shattering them…." Among the first Federals to fold were the usually stout veterans of the famed Iron Brigade, who broke and ran for the first time in their career. Their retreat triggered mass confusion in the Union ranks, halting Wadsworth's assault.

While most of Gordon's men had peeled away for their sudden flank attacks, two of his regiments did drive forward into Stone's mired men, who, like the Iron Brigade, fell back in chaos. Many wound up as prisoners.

Up and down Wadsworth's line, survivors of the failed advance tumbled back toward Ellwood, where they mingled with survivors from Griffin's advance across Saunders Field. Large groups of soldiers, said one Union officer, crowded the area and came "pouring out of the woods in great confusion and almost panic stricken." In the open ground around the Lacy house, they began to construct a log breastwork. Confederates soon appeared and were rebuffed only after a sharp firefight, bolstered on the Federal side by artillery posted on the ridge near the house.

Federal soldiers who fell back around Ellwood began constructing log breastworks for protection.

Confederate Lieutenant General A. P. Hill.

Union Brigadier General Samuel Crawford.

As Gordon's men returned from their advance, ten or twenty Georgians under Major James Van Valkenburg stumbled upon a regiment of Pennsylvanians who'd been sent to the Higgerson farm from the south to lend support to the Federal advance. Van Valkenburg tricked the two hundred and seventy-two Pennsylvanians into surrendering.

The Pennsylvanians had been sent from the nearby Chewning farm, where Federals under Brigadier General Samuel Crawford had been posted. They had marched at the head of the Federal column that morning and, when Ewell's arrival near Saunders Fields necessitated a halt, they took up position "on high ground, so that we could plainly see the store and the Orange Plank Road which runs by it," one of them later reported.

At 8:00 a.m., Crawford's men first spotted what appeared to be Confederate cavalry sparring with a detachment of Federal cavalry about a mile to the southwest at Parker's Store. Crawford sent a regiment equipped with new rapid-fire rifles to help the Federal horsemen. By 10:00, though, Crawford realized that the Confederate cavalry actually rode at the head of a large infantry force. He sent word back to Meade then, soon after, withdrew the advanced regiment. The Federal cavalry withdrew, as well.

The Confederate advance along Orange Plank Road not only brought them to the battle later than Ewell's men to the north because the road ran with more twists and turns, but it intersected the Federal position farther to the east than the north road did. That meant A. P. Hill's corps on the south road had farther to march to reach the Federals.

But when Hill finally arrived, he nearly placed the Federal army in an untenable position. The Plank Road intersected another key road, the Brock Road, and if Hill captured that intersection, he would cut the Federal army in two. Farther down the Brock Road, Winfield Scott Hancock's Second Corps was marching hard to join the rest of the Union army—but if Hancock didn't hurry, he'd find Confederates waiting for him instead.

Meade, alerted to the crisis by Crawford, bought time by directing the lead elements of John Sedgwick's Sixth Corps to hurry to the crucial intersection. Getty and his staff, riding at the vanguard of his column, arrived at the intersection at 12:30 p.m.—not a moment too soon. He could see the retreating Federal cavalry making a valiant rearguard defense, holding off the Confederate infantry as long as possible. Yet the Confederate advance down the Orange Plank Road was inexorable. "We must hold this point at any risk," Getty told his staff. "Our men will be up soon."

They arrived at a run, filing into the intersection around him. The lead brigade quickly formed into ranks and opened fire on the approaching Confederates, stymieing their advance. The Federals had won the race, but they needed to hold on until Hancock's Second Corps could arrive.

Today, remains of the Confederate earthworks stretch from the west edge of Saunders Field down to Tapp Field. Hill-Ewell Drive follows their contours.

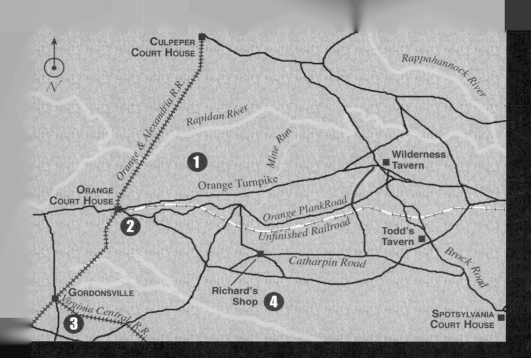

All winter, Richard Ewell's Confederate Second Corps (1) had been posted just to the west of Mine Run, with pickets stretched along the Rapidan River in case the Union Army tried to maneuver around the Confederate left flank. They could also easily occupy the old Mine Run fortifications, built the previous November and December, if the Federals chose to approach from the east. A. P. Hill's Third Corps (2) had been posted to Ewell's left, closer to Orange Court House and could respond in either direction. The locations of both corps made them ideal first responders to Grant's incursion into the Wilderness. James Longstreet's First Corps, however, had recently returned from months of service in the Western Theater and remained where they had disembarked near the railroad junction at Gordonsville (3). Lee kept them there, despite their distance from the front, because they could easily be sent to defend Richmond if the Federals moved against the Confederate capital in concert with any movement against Lee. When Lee sent Ewell and Hill to strike Grant, he originally ordered Longstreet north to Orange Court House, where the First Corps could then follow Ewell's path along the Orange Turnpike, but Longstreet suggested an alternate route that would take him toward Todd's Tavern and put him in place along the Federal flank. Lee agreed. However, because the route was so long, and because no one apprised Longstreet of the urgency of the situation in the Wilderness, he was rerouted along a shortcut from Richard's Shop (4) through the woods and onto the Orange Plank Road, which led him into the heart of the battle. Longstreet's postwar critics would try to make much of Longstreet's delay, but the "Old Warhorse" was simply following a route Lee himself, for good reason, had approved.

Crawford, meanwhile, held his position at Chewning farm as Confederates passed to the south. When he heard fighting erupt to the north—Wadsworth's general advance —he sent half of his division to help. Shortly thereafter, he recognized the vulnerability of his own position. Confederates could approach him not only from the south but, because they had advanced so far along the Orange Plank Road, from the east as well. With Wadsworth in retreat, he had no support of his own. Sometime around 2:30 p.m., under orders from Warren, the rest of his men withdrew.

The ripple of battle would continue southward, though. Confederates, eyeing the crossroads they had lost to Getty, would suddenly find Getty bringing the fight to them. What began with shots across Saunders Field earlier in the day, then shifted into the woods around Higgerson farm, would end with a bitter struggle for the Plank Road/Brock Road intersection. Federals would maintain control of the crossroads, but they would not be able to dislodge the Confederates from the Wilderness around them.

Grant hoped all day long to launch coordinated attacks that would strain Confederate resources, but the sprawling nature of the battle across a landscape that severely inhibited movement and communication prevented any such coordination—just as Lee had expected. His decision to attack along both roads, creating that sprawl, initially caught Grant off guard and then forced him to spread his army.

As Grant began to adapt, though, his army pummeled Lee's men throughout the afternoon and evening even as the Confederates successfully kept the Federals pinned in place. Lee couldn't hope to deliver a decisive blow against the much-larger Army of the Potomac until his Old Warhorse arrived with the First Corps. Like Grant, Lee wanted to fight with all his men.

Longstreet's arrival the next morning would make that possible.

WHAT BEGAN WITH SHOTS ACROSS SAUNDERS FIELD EARLIER IN THE DAY, THEN SHIFTED INTO THE WOODS AROUND HIGGERSON FARM, WOULD END WITH A BITTER STRUGGLE FOR THE PLANK ROAD/ BROCK ROAD INTERSECTION.

CHAPTER EIGHT

CRISES ON THE PLANK ROAD

When Federals launched their early-morning attack on May 6, all that stood between them and the total collapse of the Confederate army was a small handful of cannon positioned in Tapp Field commanded by Lieutenant Colonel William Poague. The artillery pieces that sit there today are actually placed a couple hundred feet farther east than where Poague had posted them.

The Orange Plank Road might have been a teeter-totter on May 5 and 6, 1864. First one crisis, then another, tipped the balance of battle one way, then the other. While sporadic fighting still erupted elsewhere on the battlefield, the emphasis of both army commanders shifted to the Plank Road and the slaughter that see-sawed back and forth.

Federals faced the first crisis. Confederates approached the Plank Road/Brock Road crossroads, threatening to prevent the Federal army from uniting its two wings. Grant and Meade, back at Ellwood, learned of the impeding crisis and ordered Brigadier General George Getty to rush his men to the intersection. Getty's infantry won the race to the cross-roads—barely. "The distance was nearly two miles, and part of the road was narrow and muddy, but the command pressed rapidly forward and reached the crossing just in time," wrote one of Getty's Vermonters. "We were not a minute too soon." Confederates, within a few hundred yards of the intersection, withdrew when the Vermonters opened fire.

Getty's Confederate counterpart, Major General Henry Heth, had been given discretionary orders from Lee to "occupy the Brock Road if you could do so without bringing on a general engagement." Heth had been under similar orders the previous July, on an excursion into the town of Gettysburg, Pennsylvania, where he had allowed himself to get drawn into

Union Brigadier
General George Getty.

Confederate Major
General Henry Heth.

a fight that evolved into the largest battle in the history of the continent. Unsure about the size of the Federal force he faced at the Brock Road intersection, and whether contact would trigger a general engagement, Heth opted not to make an issue of it.

Getty would have been willing to leave well enough alone, too, perhaps, but orders arrived from Meade for him to attack. Although Getty didn't know it, Heth outnumbered him, so when they advanced, Getty's men quickly got the worst of it. It was, said a North Carolinian, "a butchery pure and simple."

But filing in behind Getty came the Second Corps of Major General Winfield Scott Hancock—the portion of the army that would have been cut off had Confederates captured the intersection. Hancock had marched that morning south from Chancellorsville toward Todd's Tavern but, as the situation at the Wilderness began to boil, Meade ordered him to march north and reinforce Getty at the intersection.

One of the first of Hancock's units into the fray, the brigade of Brigadier General Alexander Hays, suffered severely, taking 1,390 casualties, the most of any Federal brigade during the battle. Among the killed—Hays himself, shot from his horse by a bullet to the head.

"The woods light up with the flashes of musketry as if with lightning," wrote a New Yorker in Hays' brigade, "while the incessant roar of the volleys sound like the crashing of thunderbolts." Back at the Lacy farm, Union commanders could hear the battle building toward a crescendo that would take all afternoon to peak.

More Federals poured in from the Second Corps, but the Wilderness continued to blunt their numerical advantage. "When we reached the junction of the roads, we saw the most awful confusion reigning," observed one Mainer. "Numerical superiority was seen here at its worst. There were more troops than could be utilized, almost a huddle. The roads are narrow and the woods and underbrush very dense. It was a dreadfully mixed-up mess."

Lee countered the Federal build-up by shifting more of Hill's corps into the fight. One of his divisions, that of Major General Cadmus Wilcox, had been assigned to stretch north from the Orange Plank Road to hook up with Ewell's line. Lee rerouted Wilcox's men, though, to reinforce Heth.

Throughout the rest of the afternoon, the battle teetered back and forth. Confederates came within thirty yards of capturing the intersection, but by five o'clock, they'd been edged back. By 7:30 p.m., they faced disaster of their own when a Federal unit nearly flanked them; the timely action of a brigade of North Carolinians stopped the Federal movement.

Union Major General Winfield Scott Hancock.

Lee had committed all the men he had available to the battle along the Orange Plank Road. So, when the division of Union Brigadier General James Wadsworth appeared from the northwest—after it had reorganized following its retreat from the field earlier in the afternoon—Lee must have felt his heart sink. Wadsworth's men moved through the very gap in the Confederate line Lee had created when he reassigned Wilcox's men. The Federals angled directly toward the unprotected flank of the Confederate position.

And Lee had no one he could send to stop them.

Lee quickly assembled some one hundred and fifty Alabamians who'd been assigned to guard Federal prisoners in the rear. The Alabamians "went in with a cheer," a soldier wrote—hitting the unsuspecting federals in the flank—"and whatever was before them was driven back." A single battalion had stopped Wadsworth's entire disheartened division.

The fighting along the Orange Plank Road had been "a mere slugging match in a dense thicket of small growth," said one Confederate, "where men but a few yards apart fired through the brushwood for hours, ceasing only when exhaustion and night commanded a rest."

Both exhaustion and night seemed to set in simultaneously. By 9:00 p.m., both sides settled in. "We lay upon the ground surrounded by dead and dying rebel soldiers," wrote a Wisconsin private. "The sufferings of these poor men, and their moans and cries were harrowing. We gave them water from our canteens and all aid that was within our power."

Confederates threw up a series of breastworks that snaked through the woods.

Another soldier felt haunted by the "the terrible groans of the wounded, the mournful sound of the owl and the awful shrill shrieks of the whippoorwill.... These birds seemed to mock at our grief and laugh at the groans of the dying."

Confederates threw up a piecemeal line of haphazard earthworks. Heth suggested to Hill that they take the opportunity to straighten and strengthen that line, which wound through the deep forest "like a worm fence, at every angle." Hill demurred, expecting Longstreet's First Corps to arrive at any moment. "I don't propose that your division shall do any fighting tomorrow," Hill told his anxious subordinate. He ordered Heth to rest his men, who had marched and fought all day long. Heth asked Hill to reconsider. "Damn it, Heth, I don't want to hear any more about it," Hill barked. "The men shall not be disturbed."

But Longstreet would not arrive until morning. The Old Warhorse, who had much ground to cover, had not realized how urgently Lee needed his men on the field. Now aware of the need for haste, Longstreet pushed them. Until he arrived, Lee had no one else to call on; every man then available to Ewell and Hill had been committed.

And so Lee eyed the Orange Plank Road nervously, waiting for Longstreet's arrival from the west and fearing Grant's arrival from beyond Hill's line to the east.

Grant would arrive first.

The Federal commander, who had tried throughout May 5 to launch coordinated attacks against the Confederates, felt encouraged by the day's action along the Orange Plank Road. His army had averted a potential crisis there early in the day and, by continually exerting pressure, had nearly precipitated a crisis for the Confederates. He decided to focus his army's energy there the next morning.

The Federals launched their assault just before 5:00 a.m., routing Hill's exhausted and poorly entrenched men with a rush of noise and gunfire. "The roar of musketry, the dying groans of the wounded, the hellish yells of the rebels, and the shouts and cheers of the Union men, mingle together, all making a noise and confusion that is hard to describe," a Michigander said.

"[W]e are driving them most beautifully," an exuberant Hancock reported. His assault pushed Confederates back more than a mile. Many tried to resist, but the Federal juggernaut could not be stopped. "The pressure," said a South Carolinian, "was irresistible."

As the Federal push reached the clearing around the Widow Tapp farm, a row of artillery, perched on a ridge in the field and commanded by Lieutenant Colonel William T. Poague, opened on the blue-clad soldiers. Poague and his

Grant and Meade were near Warren's headquarters at Ellwood when they learned of the crisis along the Plank Road.

Longstreet's corps, with Texans in the vanguard, arrived in time to stave off disaster for the Confederates. Lee tried to lead them into place, but they refused to advance into the fight with Lee in harm's way. "Lee to the rear!" they cried.

cannon—between twelve and sixteen of them—were all that stood between the Army of Northern Virginia and utter defeat.

Just as the crisis nearly peaked, James Longstreet's men swept onto the field. "Who are you, my boys?" Lee inquired. "Texas boys!" the men shouted back. "I am glad to see it," Lee said. He helped direct the men into position, then prepared to personally lead them into battle. "Lee to the rear!" the men began to cry. "We won't go on unless you go back!"

Lee acceded to their wishes and moved away. The men of the Lone Star State rushed forward as Lee said, admiringly, "Texans always move them!" The cost to the Texans would be high: they would lose almost two-thirds of their strength moving back the Federal advance.

The rest of Longstreet's men formed up and pushed into battle after the Texans. The Confederate crisis on the Orange Plank Road had been averted by Longstreet's nick-of-time arrival—much as the Federal crisis had been averted the previous day by the similar nick-of-time arrival of Getty's troops.

The fight along the Orange Plank Road would continue throughout the day to see-saw back and forth, but neither

Aside from the "Lee to the Rear" marker, two other monuments sit in the eastern-most corner of Tapp Field along the Orange Plank Road. One of them, made of red granite, was erected by the state of Texas to commemorate the 100th anniversary of the battle. However, the large quartz rock that lies nearby is actually the oldest marker on the site. Local citizens placed it there sometime around September 1891 to commemorate the "Lee to the Rear" incident.

James Power Smith, a Presbyterian minister who had worked on Stonewall Jackson's staff, placed a granite monument in Tapp Field to mark the area where one of the battle's most dramatic scenes took place.

side faced the kind of potentially catastrophic crisis they'd each just weathered.

For Lee, though, a different sort of calamity loomed—one that would certainly tip the balance against him and his army in the months to come.

And the calamity would feel hauntingly familiar.

The Death and Memory of Alexander Hays

Union Brigadier General Alexander Hays.

"This morning was beautiful," wrote Brigadier General Alexander Hays on May 4, 1864, in a letter to his wife. "It might have been an appropriate harbinger of the day of the regeneration of mankind, but it only brought to remembrance, through the throats of many bugles, the duty enjoined upon each one, perhaps before the setting sun, to lay down a life for his country."

It would be the last letter Hays would write to his wife. The next afternoon, on May 5, Hays would die in the battle that swirled around the Brock Road/Plank Road intersection.

But Hays' death would later serve as a symbol of the "regeneration" he'd hoped for. In June 1905, surviving members of 63rd Pennsylvania Infantry, Hays' original unit, dedicated a monument to their fallen general in the vicinity where he was killed.

At the dedication ceremony Reverend John H. Light "beseeched divine blessing for the movement to heal the wounds of war." Speaker John T. Goolrick, a local judge and Confederate veteran, condemned Southerners who, even then, forty-one years after the war, tried to keep sectional tensions alive. Goolrick promised that the Confederate people—especially veterans and their sons—would protect the Hays monument and, every Memorial Day, would decorate it. W.S. Embrey, who'd served in the Confederate army as a major, owned the land where the monument had been raised, and he presented the title for the parcel to the Pennsylvanians.

For their part, the Pennsylvanians also made an effort toward reconciliation. On their way to the dedication ceremony, they stopped at the Chancellorsville battlefield to pay their respects to Confederate General "Stonewall" Jackson, who'd fallen there in May 1863. Following the dedication of the Hays Memorial, the veterans also contributed nearly one thousand dollars toward the Confederate cemetery fund.

In 1959, the National Park Service took possession of the 0.6-acre parcel where the Hays Memorial stands. The site of Hays' death, however, took place in the woods a bit to the west.

"I am not surprised that he met his death at the head of his troops; it was just like him," said Hays' friend, Ulysses Grant. "He was a man who would never follow, but would always lead in battle."

In death, Hays' memory also served to set the good example.

CHAPTER NINE

HORROR IN THE FOREST

The forest was so dense, and the battle so intense, that bullets and cannonballs shaved off the tops of small trees.

"Danger is far less formidable in the bright, open, ventilated field, than in the dark, close wood," wrote J.F.J. Caldwell, an infantryman from South Carolina; "and it is the experience of every Confederate soldier that we fought more cheerfully where we could see our enemies, were they never so numerous, than where they could creep upon us and deal their blows invisible."

That dread, that creeping dread, lurked everywhere in the Wilderness, a terrible landscape that oppressed soldiers from both sides. The thickets grew so dense "that it was next to impossible to force one's way through them without the loss of cap and tearing of clothing," said a Union soldier from Massachusetts.

Marshes, often hidden, haunted the low spots of the terrain and sucked at the living and the dead alike. "The great, dark woods are filled with dead and wounded from both sides," wrote a soldier from Maine. "Blue and Gray sink side-by-side in its gloomy thickets and slimy pools."

Soldiers never knew when they'd stumble across a body or stumble into the enemy. Many had trouble just staying in contact with the men to the left and right of them. "The density of the woods rendered it impossible to maintain a regular line of battle," said a captain from Pennsylvania, "so we commenced bushwacking with the enemy on a grand scale." Another soldier likened it to "Indian warfare."

While popular art prints depicted the Battle of the Wilderness as an orderly, romanticized affair, the dense woods created a confusion and horror soldiers had never before experienced.

In that fashion, infantryman John McClure of Indiana found himself in a deadly game of cat-and-mouse with a Confederate. "I hid behind a tree and looked out," McClure wrote. "Across the way…was a rebel aiming at me. I put my hat on a stick…and stuck it out from behind the tree—as bait. Then I saw him peep out of the thicket and I shot him." McClure, a veteran used to fighting and killing, wasn't so used to experiencing it so intimately. "It was the first time I'd ever seen the man I'd killed, and it was an awful feeling," he said.

All around them battle raged, but many men could only tell by the sounds that roared around them, not by anything they could see. "The rattle of musketry would swell into a continuous roar as the simultaneous discharge of 10,000 guns mingled in one grand concert, and then after a few minutes, became more interrupted, resembling the crash of some huge king of the forest when felled by the stroke of the woodsman's ax," wrote a New Yorker. "Then would be heard the wild yells which always told of a rebel charge, and again the volleys would swell into one continuous roll of sound, which would

presently be interrupted by the vigorous manly cheers of the northern soldiers…which indicated a repulse of their enemies."

Sounds of chaos echoed everywhere. "I could almost hear the confusion of contending armies," a Michigander wrote. "I could almost hear the shrieks of the wounded & the dying, the picture of upturned faces pale and motionless, sleeping their last sleep amid the roar of battle…. There was something horrible about this wholesale slaughter of man by man. I could hardly realize that a great battle was raging within a short distance from me."

The chaos came in many shapes. One Pennsylvanian had a snake drop on him from a cedar tree. "The sergent jumped and scampered around in much fright paying no attention to the Bullets," a witness said. "The snake took to the grass and di(s)appeared from view. The Sergent thought he could stand a few bullets, but when they commenced shooting Snakes it was time to Stampede."

The woods caught fire in a dozen places, forcing soldiers to scramble to save fallen comrades.

Soldiers from both sides worked together to rescue wounded men trapped by the flames.

Men did things under those trying circumstances they otherwise wouldn't have imagined. One Union soldier saw a group of Confederates build a line of fortifications out of dead bodies: They "would lay a pile of dead men along then dig a trench and throw the dirt over the bodies serving the double purpose of burying their dead and building breastworks."

Worst of all, perhaps, were the fires. Though the forest itself was lush and green, the dead leaves and detritus of the previous autumn lay ankle deep on the forest floor. Sparks from gunfire set the woods ablaze in a dozen places. "Hundreds of wounded on both sides, unable to crawl away from the swiftly approaching flames, could only lay and moan and roast and die," recalled a Union engineer. Between the lines, said another Union soldier, "these fires spread unchecked over acres, disfiguring beyond possibility of recognition the bodies of the killed and proving fatal to hundreds of helpless wounded men who lay there looking for the friendly aid which never came and who died at last the victims of the relentless flames."

Cartridge boxes still strapped to the dead and wounded exploded in the flames, blowing "ghastly holes" in the bellies and sides of bodies. "The almost cheerful 'Pop! Pop!' of cartridges gave no hint of the almost dreadful horror their noise bespoke," said a New York Zouave. "The bodies of the dead were blackened and burned beyond all possibility of recognition."

Field hospitals, flooded with wounded men, became charnel houses.

One artillerist saw a soldier with two broken legs "lying on the ground with his cocked rifle by his side and his ramrod in his hand, and his eyes set on the front. I know he meant to kill himself in case of fire—knew it as surely as though I could read his thoughts."

"To add to the miseries of the battle," recalled the Union engineer, "no water could be found as no springs or running brooks were in the Wilderness. Many died from thirst, many from excitement and sun-stroke."

And so, as war raged, so did the fires—the smoke from the fight comingling with the smoke from the flames. "The smoke from the clouds of powder and the denser clouds caused by the burning woods became stifling, suffocating, blinding," the engineer said. "Two hundred thousand men, inspired with the desperation of demons, were fighting in a wilderness of fire."

The wounded who could move fought their way through the Wilderness to the rear. "[A] continued stream of faint and bleeding humanity was pouring back from the reeking front, staining the fresh young blades of grass into torrents of blood," said one Union soldier. Federals had established their field hospitals near Ellwood, at Wilderness Tavern and near the intersection of the Germanna Plank Road and Orange Turnpike. Confederates had established hospitals near

"THE CAMPAIGN IS THE
SEVEREST ONE EVER
ENDURED BY ANY ARMY
IN THE WORLD."

—FEDERAL OFFICER
WHO FOUGHT AT THE
WILDERNESS.

Parker's Store along the Orange Plank Road and near Locust Grove and Robinson's Tavern along the Orange Turnpike. Surgeons of both armies worked desperately to save as many as they could. "Amputating tables groaned with fainting sufferers and the surgeon's knife was plied unceasingly," the soldier said. "The scene was sickening and terrible, even as much so as the awful carnage of battle which still raged on like a carnival of hell not two miles distant."

These same two armies, only a year earlier, had fought through this same Wilderness during the battle of Chancellorsville. On the third day of that battle, a portion of the woods had even caught fire. But the close-quarters dread of the Wilderness seemed to overshadow the earlier fight. It was like fighting "in the shadow of death," said one of Grant's staff officers.

And whereas the armies at Chancellorsville fought intensely then disengaged, the Wilderness served as the opening of a brawl that would last all summer and cover hundreds of miles. "The campaign is the severest one ever endured by any army in the world," said one Federal officer. Plenty of men on both sides agreed with him.

"A soldier I once met asked me where I was wounded," recalled Colonel Selden Connor of Maine years after the war, "and on my replying 'In the Wilderness' he responded 'Humph! Anybody could get hit there.'"

A scene of "unutterable horror"

In his memoir *Campaigning with Grant*, Horace Porter, a member of Grant's staff, said there were features of the Battle of the Wilderness "which have never been matched in the annals of warfare":

All circumstances seemed to combine to make the scene one of unutterable horror. At times the wind howled through the tree-tops, mingling its moans with the groans of the dying, and heavy branches were cut off by the fire of the artillery, and fell crashing upon the heads of the men, adding a new terror to battle. Forest fires raged; ammunition trains exploded; the dead were roasted in the conflagration; the wounded, roused by its hot breath, dragged themselves along with their torn and mangled limbs, in the mad energy of despair, to escape the ravages of the flames; and every bush seemed hung with shreds of blood-stained clothing. It seems as though Christian men had turned to fiends, and hell itself had usurped the place of earth.

"All circumstances seemed to combine to make the scene one of unutterable horror," remembered Horace Porter, a member of Grant's staff.

The 6th Corps, Battle of the Wilderness, fighting in the woods

CHAPTER TEN

CONFEDERATES UNLEASHED

Confederates launched an early morning assault north of Saunders Field against the Federal Sixth Corps just minutes before the Federals were scheduled to launch an assault of their own. To the south, along the Orange Plank Road, Federals initiated an attack that caught Confederates off guard.

It had all gone so well, and then it had all gone so wrong.

Seizing the initiative by attacking first, just before dawn, the Federals had rolled back the entire right wing of the Confederate army. Then, the sudden appearance of the Confederate First Corps knocked the assault back on its heels. Federals stubbornly resisted, but James Longstreet hammered them back, back, back. "[N]ever did his great qualities as a tenacious, fighting soldier shine forth in better light," said his chief of staff.

Along the Orange Turnpike to the north, a 5:00 a.m. assault planned by the Federal Sixth Corps was preempted when Richard Ewell's Confederates attacked first. "Ewell's watch must be fifteen minutes ahead," noted Sixth Corps commander John Sedgwick. A Georgian offered a different reason. "[W]e had the enemy entirely in our power and were eager to begin the fray," he boasted. The Confederate attack, although not especially powerful, served to throw off any hope of a Federal offensive along the Turnpike—especially by Gouverneur Warren, entrenched to the south of Sedgwick, who refused to take the offensive despite orders to do so.

By midmorning, reports reached Lee that the left end of the Federal line south of the Orange Plank Road was unprotected. Longstreet quickly organized an assault force to move through the forest and along an unfinished railroad cut, then circle around to hit the Union flank.

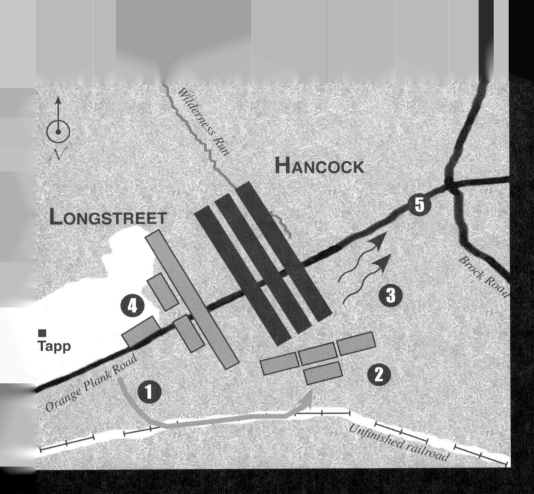

At 11:00, Longstreet sent four brigades along an unfinished railroad trace (1), which put Confederates in position along the Union left flank (2). The flank attack, launched at the same time Longstreet launched an attack along his front, caused the Union position to crumble (3). Longstreet followed up by sending Brigadier General Micah Jenkins' brigade straight up the middle (4), but during that attack Longstreet was accidentally wounded by his own men. The Union Second Corps used the resulting delay to set up a defensive position at the Brock Road/Plank Road intersection (5).

James Wadsworth, shot in the head while trying to stave off Longstreet's assault, was carried to a Confederate field hospital. He died two days later.

"It was like an army of ghosts rising out of the earth," one Federal officer recalled. Yet those ghosts hit "[l]ike an avalanche from a mountain side," a Confederate said. First one, then another and another Federal brigade collapsed under the Confederate sweep, which turned the Wilderness into a "vast, weird, horrible slaughter pen." A Vermonter ruefully watched his men fall back around him. "All organization and control seemed to have been lost," he wrote.

As the flanking force swept in, Longstreet executed a perfectly timed frontal assault in concert with it. "Longstreet intended to play his hand for all it was worth, & to push the pursuit with his whole force," wrote a Confederate observer.

Federal division commander James Wadsworth, on the Orange Plank Road, tried to staunch the flow of retreating men while also trying to fend off Longstreet's assault. In the mêlée, he led a doomed countercharge down the road—"It is certain death," a subordinate proclaimed as he ordered his men to follow—but unable to make headway, he ordered his men back. As he did, Wadsworth lost control of his horse, which bolted toward the Confederates. They shot Wadsworth in the head. For the rest of the afternoon, Confederates traveling the road noticed the white-haired general, propped uncomfortably against a tree along the roadside, barely clinging to life. They rifled through his pockets. Wadsworth would

Confederates moved along an unfinished railroad cut to slip around the Union left flank.

never regain consciousness and died in a Confederate field hospital on May 8.

Longstreet, too, would meet a grim fate only moments later. He rode at the head of a column of fresh troops, advancing toward the newly established Federal position at the Brock Road/Plank Road intersection. One of his staff officers suggested to the general that he was exposing himself too much. "That is our business," Longstreet replied.

Just then elements of the flanking column mistook Longstreet's party for Union soldiers and fired upon them. Longstreet took a bullet through the neck and shoulder. Although it didn't kill him, the wound removed him from the fight.

Longstreet's wounding necessitated a halt in the Confederate advance while officers reorganized, although Longstreet tried to urge them on. "Tell [General Lee]," he said in a choked whisper, "that the enemy were in utter rout, and if pressed, would all be his before night."

A messenger who brought the news to Lee said, "I shall not soon forget the sadness in his face, and the almost despairing movement of his hands, when he was told Longstreet had fallen."

"Could we have pushed forward at once, I believe Grant's army would have been routed," wrote Major General Charles

Field, the officer who took command in Longstreet's stead. But, Field pointed out, pushing forward at once was impossible. He ordered the flanking force to realign itself with the rest of the Confederate line in order to prevent further calamities.

It took hours to reorganize, and the delay provided Federals with enough time to construct three lines of breastworks around the intersection. They turned it into "one of the strongest lines of temporary works it had ever been my fortune to stand behind," said a New Yorker.

Despite the loss of his Old War Horse, Lee resolved to maintain the initiative along the Plank Road. Shortly after 4:00 p.m., he ordered an attack against the Union position. Unfortunately, said a Confederate officer, "it seemed more like an apology for the attack Longstreet was conducting, than anything really calculated to produce results."

Confederate Major General Charles Field.

The Federals, reorganized and protected by their works, succeeded in repulsing most of the advances, but when the spreading forest fires ignited the logs of the earthworks, it "added renewed terrors and excitement to the situation," said a Federal officer. Confederates exploited the opening, charging like "devils through the flames" into the Federal lines.

"I saw a rebel officer mount the rampart with a flag in his hand, waving it over the heads of his men," recalled that same Federal officer. "As the rebel flag was flaunting over the burning ramparts, [a] brigade came sweeping up at the double quick, and with a wild hurrah drove the rebels back into the mass of flames and smoke and recovered everything that had been temporarily lost."

At that moment, the Union Ninth Corps, commanded by Major General Ambrose Burnside, appeared on the field in a position to threaten the Confederate left. Confederates countered, but the action effectively ended fighting along the Orange Plank Road.

But Lee wasn't finished.

From north of the Orange Turnpike, news arrived that the right flank of the Union army also appeared vulnerable. Neither Meade nor Grant had apparently learned a lesson about protecting the army's flanks, so Confederates resolved

A Vermonter swept up in Longstreet's flank attack called the collapse of the Federal position a "terrific tempest of disaster." Today, a monument made of Vermont granite stands at the spot where soldiers from the Green Mountain State saw some of their heaviest fighting.

Federals had time to construct formidable breastworks, but even those powerful defenses couldn't withstand the forest fires that raged through the woods.

to teach the lesson again. After some debate with his officers, Ewell authorized Brigadier General John Brown Gordon to mount a flanking attack at the northernmost edge of the battlefield.

Gordon launched his attack as dusk settled over the deep woods, which would eventually make it impossible for him to maintain effective communication and coordination. At its outset, though, the attack crushed the Union opposition. "The scene was instantly a very pandemonium of sights and sounds," said one soldier. "The crashing of the timber under the artillery fire, the rolling volleys, the rattling…fire, the commands and cheers of our people and the fierce Rebel yell filled the air with sounds, while the hand-to-hand encounters, the clubbed musket and the bayonet were brought into play."

"They swung around to our rear, and we had more than we could take care of," said a New Yorker. The Sixth Corps fell back, but their commander, Sedgwick, soon rallied them along a narrow road. "Halt! For God's sake, boys, rally!" Sedgwick bellowed. "Don't disgrace yourselves and your general this way!"

Word of the Confederate assault reached Grant at about the same time darkness brought an end to the fighting. "Had there been daylight," Grant later wrote, "the enemy could

have injured us very much in the confusion that prevailed."

Thus ended the second day of fighting in the Wilderness. Grant had sought to push Confederates with a series of strong, coordinated attacks, but Lee upended those plans by exercising the initiative for most of the day—"not because Lee had obviously the best of it," observed one of Grant's staffers, "but because [Grant] himself had discovered the Army of the Potomac's one weakness, the lack of springy formation, and audacious, self-reliant initiative."

It proved to be an invaluable lesson for the general from out west, who would soon demonstrate himself to be a quick learner.

Taking advantage of the fire, Confederates broke through the Union defenses at the Brock Road before being driven back.

Confederate Brigadier General John B. Gordon (left) led a late-afternoon flank attack against the Union Sixth Corps, commanded by Major General John Sedgwick (right), at the northernmost end of the battlefield. The engagement marked the last major fighting of the battle.

Longstreet's Wounding

The story of James Longstreet's wounding in the Wilderness is frequently eclipsed by a similar incident a year earlier: the accidental wounding of Thomas Jonathan "Stonewall" Jackson during the Battle of Chancellorsville.

One year and four days prior to Longstreet's wounding, on May 2, 1863, less than four miles away, Jackson sustained mortal injuries when his men accidentally opened fire on him as he engaged in a nighttime reconnaissance.

While the specific circumstances differed, there were still many parallels. Both men were lieutenant generals. Both had overseen highly successful flanking maneuvers around a superior Union foe.

Also like Jackson, Longstreet was looking to follow up on his victory and keep momentum rolling. Longstreet and his staff rode forward at the head of a fresh brigade, the men "dressed in new uniforms made of cloth so dark a gray as to be almost black," said one Confederate. Their brigade commander, Brigadier General Micah Jenkins, encouraged his men to cheer as they prepared to enter battle.

Longstreet and the cheering column of dark-garbed soldiers traveled east on the Orange Plank Road just as Confederates, finishing off their flanking movement, approached the road through the woods on the road's right side. Those men, "some distance off in the thick underbrush, hearing the cheers and seeing this body of dark uniformed men, took them for Yankees and fired a volley," said a Confederate officer.

Across the way, more of the flanking Confederates, who'd already crossed the road, gotten lost, and were groping their way back to the main Confederate line, thought the gunfire was directed at them, so they returned fire.

Thus, Longstreet and his staff found themselves caught in a sudden crossfire between two Virginia regiments—the 12th and the 41st—who'd mistaken each other for Union troops in the forest.

James Longstreet, photographed after the war. His right arm, tucked into his unbuttoned jacket, remained unusable for the rest of his life because of the injury he sustained in the Wilderness.

Bullets killed Jenkins, a staff officer, and a courier. Longstreet took a bullet through the neck. The exit wound, through his right shoulder, would rob him of the use of his arm for the rest of his life. "Longstreet, who had stood there like a lion at bay, reeled as the blood poured down over his breast, and was evidently badly hurt," a witness said.

Officers quelled the confusion, and Confederates on both sides of the road looked on in horrified astonishment at what they'd done. At least one witness thought the casualty list

Riding at the head of an advancing column of Confederates, Longstreet and his men found themselves in the middle of a firefight triggered by mistaken identity.

could have been worse. "Fortunately they fired high, or there would have been a terrible slaughter," he said. "As it was...the effect was horrible."

The initial prognosis for Longstreet looked dire. His staff soon placed him into an ambulance and moved him to a field hospital in the rear, near Parker's Store. "The blood had paled out of his face and its somewhat gross aspect was gone," said a Confederate artillerist who looked in on the general. "I noticed how white and dome-like his great forehead looked and, with scarcely less reverent admiration, how spotless white his socks and his fine gauze undervest, save where the black red gore from his breast and shoulder had stained it...."

Comparisons to Jackson's ill fate proved inevitable. "By some strange fatality the flank movement, patterned after Jackson's of the year before in the same vicinity, had had the same brilliant success in routing the enemy in a panic, & the same melancholy termination..." wrote a Confederate officer.

"Heaven grant that Lee may not lose his left arm now, as he lost his right arm then!" wrote a newspaper correspondent.

"It seems almost impossible to prevent blunders of this kind during the excitement and confusion of a battle in such a place where…the contending forces are fighting unseen foes even when at short range and almost face to face," said a Confederate cavalryman.

In his memoirs, Ulysses Grant acknowledged that Longstreet's wounding had an impact on the battle. "His loss was a severe one to Lee," Grant wrote, "and compensated in a great measure for the mishap, or misapprehensions, which had fallen to our lot during the day."

While Longstreet's wounding had an immediate impact on the battle, Lee would come to understand the real ramifications of the accident in the weeks to come. With Longstreet gone, Lee faced a leadership crisis in his army. He had no one to fill the void left by Longstreet's absence—which would lead to serious negative consequences as the summer of '64 wore on.

"[T]he evil genius of the South is still hovering over those desolate woods," a Confederate wrote, evoking the accidents that wounded both Jackson and Longstreet. "We almost seem to be struggling against destiny itself."

"[T]HE EVIL GENIUS OF THE SOUTH IS STILL HOVERING OVER THOSE DESOLATE WOODS," A CONFEDERATE WROTE, EVOKING THE ACCIDENTS THAT WOUNDED BOTH JACKSON AND LONGSTREET.

Where's Burnside?

Union Major General Ambrose Burnside.

Today, Major General Ambrose P. Burnside is best known for his extravagant facial hair. In 1864, the affable Burnside was best known among his peers for his "genius for slowness."

Burnside had once commanded the Army of the Potomac, but after the debacle at Fredericksburg, Virginia, in December of 1862, followed by the disastrous "Mud March" the following January, Burnside resigned. The whiskered general assumed command of his old Ninth Corps, and together they shuffled from assignment to assignment—including a contest against James Longstreet's detached corps at Knoxville, Tennessee, in November of 1863.

When Grant assumed command of all Union armies, he recalled the Ninth Corps from Tennessee. Because Burnside outranked Major General George Gordon Meade, commander of the Army of the Potomac, Grant could not incorporate the Ninth Corps into the army without ruffling feathers. Nonetheless, Grant moved the Ninth Corps in concert with the Army of the Potomac, issuing orders to Burnside that worked in tandem with the orders Grant issued Meade.

Things went wrong almost from the beginning.

On May 4, the Ninth Corps brought up the rear of the advancing Federal column. On May 5, when battle erupted, Grant ordered Burnside to support Warren along the Orange Turnpike. Burnside never made it into position even though his corps was only a short march away.

That night, Burnside met with Meade and the army's other corps commanders. When ordered to break camp at 2:00 a.m. the following morning, Burnside happily assured everyone that they could count on his troops to be ready to break camp "by half past two!"

Burnside's coordinated advance that next morning, on May 6, made up a crucial component of the assault Grant had ordered for 4:30 a.m. "He won't be up—I know him well," one of Meade's staff officers said. The other corps commanders agreed, so they requested a slightly later start time to accommodate. Grant gave them thirty minutes—just enough of a

delay to allow Ewell to take the initiative along the Turnpike instead of Sedgwick.

Hancock, counting on Burnside's support for the morning assault along the Plank Road, had to push the attack on his own because Burnside failed to show at the appointed hour. "I knew it!" Hancock exclaimed. "Just what I expected." Burnside, it turned out, had stopped for breakfast.

"No one had expected much from Burnside," says historian Gordon Rhea, "and his failure to meet Grant's timetable was viewed as but another example of his inveterate slowness."

Also of note from the Ninth Corps, aside from Burnside's case of the slows: Members of the United States Colored Troops served with the Ninth Corps during the Battle of the Wilderness, marking the first appearance of black soldiers in the Eastern Theater. "They were fine looking men, and were anxious to have a 'hand in' as soon as possible," one observer noted. While the black soldiers did not take place in the fighting, they played a valuable role behind the scenes. As Grant's Overland Campaign continued, though, their time on the front lines would come.

Burnside had earned a reputation for his leisurely pace.

Lieut. U.S. Grant at Wilderness Va May 7th 1864.

CHAPTER ELEVEN

GRANT MOVES SOUTH

———

When Federal soldiers realized Grant intended to move south rather than retreat, they broke into a spontaneous cheer.

It would not have been an exaggeration to call it the middle of nowhere: an unremarkable crossroads in the heart of the Wilderness where the Orange Plank Road and Brock Road intersected.

By the afternoon of May 5, 1864, it would become the most important intersection in America.

For Confederates advancing from the west, the intersection represented an opportunity to wedge themselves between two wings of the Union army, catching them off guard and preventing their unification.

For Federals advancing from the southeast, the intersection represented an opportunity to block an aggressive and unexpected Confederate movement that put the Northern army in jeopardy.

But by the night of May 6, the crossroads represented far, far more.

Two days of intense fighting and blistering fire had swirled around the intersection, with neither side holding any more advantage than they'd possessed before the battle opened.

"Joe Johnston would have retreated after two days of such punishment," Ulysses S. Grant noted, calling to mind the principal general of the Confederacy's western armies. Johnston would have retreated, but Robert E. Lee kept coming and coming and coming. Lee had, in fact, successfully achieved his primary goal, striking a blow at the Federal army in a spot where the Federal army could not effectively strike back.

Burial parties sent out on May 7 to inter the dead dug shallow graves that often left remains exposed after a rainfall or two.

But Grant, too, had achieved something important. He had drawn Lee out from behind Confederate fortifications and into battle. The result, although not a tactical victory, represented a strategic one.

The last fighting of May 6 had sputtered into occasional after-dark potshots between pickets. Forest fires roared like freight trains and threw orange light and black smoke into the night. Wounded men, lost in the undergrowth, groaned and shrieked and wept. Members of Grant's and Meade's staffs, atop their knoll at the Lacy farm, could see, could hear, could smell the destruction all around them.

Grant himself, deep in thought, stared into his campfire. He wore his hat pulled low over his eyes. He had earlier abandoned his whittling, had gone into his tent to give voice to his grief, had returned with his old stoicism draped across his face to sit by the campfire and contemplate the crossroads before him.

Somewhere nearby, a band began to play. The song, familiar to all, floated down from the Lacy farm and over the battlefield and, said a Confederate, "it re-echoed through that pine forest, the old patriot air, 'The Star Spangled Banner,' and after that music had died away our band responded with that air so dear to Southern hearts, 'The Bonnie Blue Flag,' and it was responded to by 'Home, Sweet Home.'"

That's where the army would be heading soon, many Federals thought—back north, back home, back to safety, away from the indomitable Lee and the Army of Northern Virginia. Federal commanders had all found grief at Lee's hands, and all had withdrawn or, at the very least, had avoided further bludgeoning. Grant, most assumed, would act no differently now that he'd gotten his first taste of what Lee could do. "[H]e is now studying how to get back across the Rapidan," one Union soldier sneered.

Indeed, Grant knew he could not stand for more punishment in the Wilderness. "I do not hope to gain any decided advantage from the fighting in this forest," he told an aide.

Yet he knew he could not—would not—retreat. As he had told a newspaper correspondent the previous evening, there would be no turning back.

Instead, he eyed a movement to the south, around Lee's right flank. "This will, in all probability, compel him to try and throw himself between us and Richmond," he explained to an aide, "and in such a movement I hope to be able to attack him in a more open country, and outside of his breastworks."

Grant issued his order early the next morning, stressing the need for secrecy. An uneasy détente held between the two armies, with skirmishing erupting at various points along the line all day. If Lee divined Grant's intentions, he might bring on a full engagement or slide out of position and look for a way to disrupt Grant's maneuver.

But both sides seemed content to skirmish throughout the day without launching any all-out assaults. Occasionally, artillery opened fire. In the early afternoon, Confederate shells began to rain down around Ellwood. "[T]he enemy's shells fall near…Headquarters," complained Warren. Meade, at his own headquarters nearby, snapped a reply: "Well, can't

> "I DO NOT HOPE TO GAIN ANY DECIDED ADVANTAGE FROM THE FIGHTING IN THIS FOREST."
>
> –U. S. GRANT

After repulsing the Confederate attack on May 6, soldiers in the Federal Second Corps spent the night fortifying their position. By the morning of May 7, it looked formidable.

I see that? What's that to do with it?" He refused to authorize a vigorous response for fear of escalating the conflict even as preparations continued to move the army.

As part of those preparations, surgeons shuttled wounded soldiers to the rear, toward Chancellorsville, and eventually on to Fredericksburg. Supply wagons prepared to move. Cavalry rode forward to scout the way. Burial parties carried out their solemn work. Infantrymen destroyed anything the Confederates might be able to scavenge. "The arms in our possession, either captured from the enemy or belonging to our killed and wounded, were gathered up and broken or buried," said an artillerist; "and in order to deceive the enemy headboards were placed over them containing the names of fictitious soldiers."

Just after dusk, Grant rode out to the Brock Road/Plank Road crossroads. He had faced a crossroads of his own and had chosen to go forward. That road, literally, ran southeast from this intersection, which his men had fought so hard to retain control of. Now, the fruits of their work provided the Army of the Potomac a road to travel onward. This would be

no McClellan-esque "On to Richmond!" drive full of pomp
and bluster—but soldiers along the road did notice which
direction Grant was moving as he and his staff trotted past
them: "[T]he chief who had led them through the mazes of
the Wilderness was again moving forward with his horse's
head turned toward Richmond."

Their reaction was as spontaneous as it was exuberant.
"Soldiers weary and sleepy after their long battle, with stiff-
ened limbs and smarting wounds, now sprang to their feet,
forgetful of their pains, and rushed forward to the roadside,"
wrote one of Grant's staffers. "Wild cheers echoed through
the forest, and glad shouts of triumph rent the air. Men
swung their hats, tossed up their arms, and pressed forward
to within touch of their chief, clapping their hands, and
speaking to him with the familiarity of comrades."

Staffers urged the men to keep quiet in order to preserve
the secrecy Grant wanted to maintain. "[B]ut," one of them
said, "the demonstration did not really cease until the general
was out of sight."

The Army of the Potomac, for the first time in its career,
was moving forward after a battle.

Lee caught the move, and although Grant had a head
start, Lee had a smaller, faster army. With the help of his
cavalry, Lee managed to slip ahead of Grant and dictate terms
of battle. "In his renewed effort to get past our flank," wrote a
Confederate officer admiringly, "Grant gave us further experience of his qualities as a general."

From the crossroads in the Wilderness, Grant would
move his army left and to the south, left and to the south,
fighting Lee whenever he could bring on an engagement,
flanking him when he couldn't. "I propose to fight it out along
this line if it takes all summer," Grant would declare.

That line, left and to the south, would take the armies to
the outskirts of Spotsylvania Courthouse, to the steep banks
of the North Anna River and to Totopotomoy Creek, and to
the killing grounds of Cold Harbor. Then Grant would swing
south of the James River and settle into a siege around Peters-
burg. And all the time, he would hold to his original plan:

"[T]HE CHIEF WHO
HAD LED THEM
THROUGH THE MAZES
OF THE WILDERNESS
WAS AGAIN MOVING
FORWARD WITH HIS
HORSE'S HEAD TURNED
TOWARD RICHMOND."

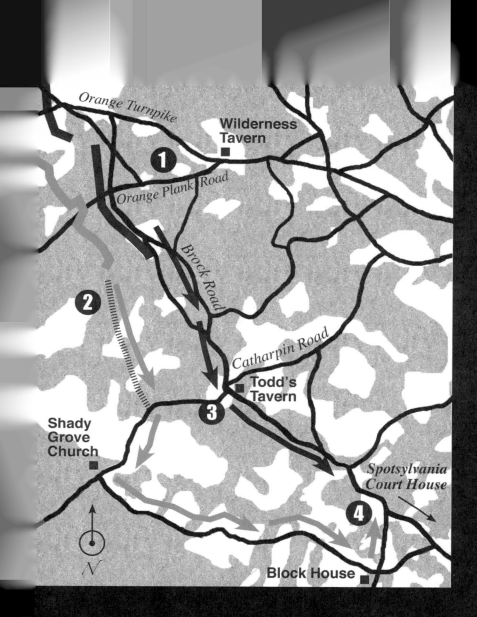

Orange Turnpike

Wilderness Tavern

① Orange Plank Road

Brock Road

② Catharpin Road

Todd's Tavern

③

Shady Grove Church

Spotsylvania Court House

④

N

Block House

On the evening of March 7, Union commander Ulysses S. Grant decided to flank the Confederate army by moving left and south. His Fifth Corps lead the way south on the Brock Road (1). Confederate commander Robert E. Lee countered by sending his First Corps southward along a road constructed through the Wilderness by his engineers (2). Confederate cavalry successfully stalled the Union advance near Todd's Tavern (3), giving the First Corps the time it needed to reach Laurel Hill on the morning of May 8 (4). The Confederates arrived just moments before the Federals, thus blocking the Union advance to Spotsylvania Court House.

On the evening of May 6, Grant faced a crossroads, both literally and figuratively. Brock Road, which led to the south, represented one of several options available to the Union commander.

hammer continuously against the armed force of the enemy and his resources, until by mere attrition, if in no other way, there should be nothing left to him."

Joshua Lawrence Chamberlain, an officer from Maine, would later observe: "The hammering business had been hard on the hammer." Grant left in his wake some 18,000 casualties in the Wilderness alone, compared to some 11,000 Confederate casualties. The names of the dead began to appear in long rolls on the front pages of newspapers, and as the Overland Campaign ground onward, Northern morale sank ever deeper and cries for an end to the war grew louder. Morale sank so low President Lincoln felt assured he would fail in his reelection bid—making himself a casualty of that same grim math he knew was necessary to win the war.

But once Grant made his choice at the crossroads in the Wilderness, once he resolved to take the road southward, direction would never again matter. It would only be a matter, then, of time before the road led to Appomattox Court House.

Lee on May 7th

Confederate Major General Richard Anderson.

As May 7 dawned, surgeons lifted James Longstreet into the back of an ambulance for the trip to Orange Court House, where a train would take him to Charlottesville to begin his long recuperation. "He is very feeble and nervous and suffers much from his wound," said an observer, although the overall prognosis looked favorable.

Lee saw his trusted lieutenant off, then set about the work of deciding upon a replacement. He had several capable officers to choose from, and in the end he settled on Major General Richard Anderson—"chivalrous, deliberate 'Dick' Anderson," as one of Longstreet's aides described him. Although not an especially brilliant strategist, Anderson performed solidly enough, and he was familiar to the men.

As morning passed into afternoon, Lee's men, entrenched in a strong line that snaked through the thick undergrowth, traded shots and forays with their Union counterparts, but Lee, "constrained to spare his men as much as possible, hesitated to assail the enemy in his intrenched [sic] position," said a Confederate officer. Instead, Lee "hopefully awaited attack." Grant had spent the previous two days trying to assume the offensive, and Lee had every reason to think he would do so again. And so Lee waited.

As the day wore on, and it became apparent Grant would not launch the attacks Lee expected, the Confederate commander began to consider the other possibilities that lay before him. If Grant didn't attack, then he would have to move—but in which direction? Retreat back across the Rapidan the way he'd come? Withdraw eastward toward Fredericksburg? Move southward toward Spotsylvania Court House? The options provided Lee with some hard choices.

To better determine Grant's intentions, Lee sent out a pair of reconnaissance forces to the north. He also ordered his engineers to construct a trail through the woods toward the south so he could move to intercept the Federals if they shifted that way.

Confederate soldiers spent the day trying to scavenge what they could from the field. Burial parties interred corpses individually in shallow graves where they fell or sometimes in communal pits the shovellers marked with crude headboards. They searched the bodies of Union dead for money and valuables. One Confederate, who hadn't eaten since before the battle, scavenged for food. "I have been so hungry that I have cut the blood off from crackers and eaten them," he complained.

By mid-afternoon, Lee began to receive reports that Grant might be preparing a move southward, toward Spotsylvania Court House. He asked his cavalry in that direction to gather more intelligence, and he prepped the newly promoted Anderson, who would lead the Confederate withdrawal, on what to do. By nightfall, the Army of Northern Virginia was on the move.

"Such were the prominent features of the entire campaign," wrote a Confederate artillerist. "It was a succession of death grapples and recoils and races for new position, and several times during the campaign the race was so close and tense and clearly defined that we could determine the exact location of the Federal column by the cloud of dust that overhung and crept along the horizon parallel to our own advance."

The race southward was on.

Confederates skirmished with Federals on and off throughout May 7 even as commanders on both sides made preparations to leave the Wilderness.

The Two Generals, Revisited

That Grant sat and whittled away the Battle of the Wilderness had less to do with his cool nerves than with his desire to let George Gordon Meade run the Army of the Potomac as Meade saw fit. It was, after all, Meade's army. Grant, as commander of all armies, could have chosen to execute his duties in an office in Washington. That he made his office in the field, with the Union's largest and most visible army, obviously led to some confusion about who was really in charge, so he made an effort to defer to Meade's judgment on all things tactical.

But as the battle wore on, and Grant finally got to see the Army of the Potomac in action firsthand, he began to understand why it had such a long legacy of underachieving. The army moved slowly. Communication was inconsistent. Corps commanders exercised wills of their own—wills that frequently demonstrated obstinacy instead of prudent caution. No one dared act with boldness.

This was a problem Meade himself had recognized. Just weeks after the Battle of Gettysburg, in July 1863, Meade wrote to his wife that "Another great trouble with me is the want of active and energetic subordinate officers, men upon whom I can depend and rely upon taking care of themselves and commands."

As institutionalized as the army's problems had become, and as much as they hinged on personalities, they still all began at the top, with competent but cautious Meade, who just couldn't seem to get his army to act.

Grant learned that lesson for himself at the Wilderness, and so afterward, he took a more direct hand in the tactical operation and maneuver of the army. The command structure proved awkward at times, and while Meade chafed under it, he never publicly protested. Quoting a newspaper account, he described it as "'the Army of the Potomac, directed by Grant, commanded by Meade, and led by Hancock, Sedgwick and Warren,' which is quite a good distinction, and about hits the nail on the head."

On May 13, Grant recommended Meade for promotion to major general in the regular army (Meade had been a major general of volunteers). "General Meade has more than met my most sanguine expectations," Grant wrote, calling Meade one of "the fittest officers for large commands I have come in contact with."

As the Overland Campaign progressed, Meade complained privately that Grant's star continually eclipsed his own. Yet he also showed genuine respect and admiration for Grant, whom he called "a good soldier, of great force of character, honest and upright, of pure purposes.... [H]e is, in my judgment, the best man the war has yet produced."

The relationship between Meade and Grant evolved as the Overland Campaign progressed. Although Meade respected his commander, he also felt overshadowed by him.

EPILOGUE

Despite the postwar
depression in the South,
Ellwood was again a
profitable farm by the
mid-1870s.

The salmon-colored house on the crest of the hill at the heart
of the Lacy plantation, Ellwood, stood vacant for eight years
after the war ended. Surviving records suggest that the house
remained uninhabitable for a time and that the Lacys then
rented out the farm for a spell. A carpetbagger, hoping in vain
that the property would be confiscated, may have squatted in
the building for a time, too.

But by 1872, after selling their grand home, Chatham, to
settle debts, the Lacys moved from Fredericksburg to take up
permanent residence in their country estate. Only two of their
former slaves remained with them.

Despite the postwar depression that afflicted the South,
the Lacys once again transformed their farm into a profitable
enterprise.

Two newspaper correspondents, traveling across Virginia
in the summer of 1879, paid a visit to Ellwood at Lacy's invi-
tation. The land they found hardly resembled the dark, close
wood of the war years. "We saw nothing particularly 'wild,'
'weird,' or 'howling,' about the Wilderness," they wrote:

*It was not the most interesting country, to be sure. But the
blackberries were the finest we had eaten, the green apples
the sourest; the houses were whitewashed and neatly kept;
flowers were tenderly reared by even the poorest and plainest
of the people...the roads good; and all things wearing a thrifty,
peaceful, and happy aspect....*

The Higgerson house survived until 1938, when it burned to the ground, leaving only the chimney behind.

Here in the autonomy of Ellwood, situated in a beautiful valley and extending in some directions as far as the eye could reach, our genial host entertained us in a way that…would never associate with the 'weird shadows and the awful gloom' of the Wilderness.

Two years earlier, in 1877, the unfinished railroad that ran between Fredericksburg and Orange Court House had finally been completed. The train traveling the narrow-gauge line stopped in the hamlet of Parker's Store—although, by that time, the store itself was no more. Two other general stores sprang up in the area, though, along with a post office, a wagon shop, and a pair of lumber dealers.

Nearby, the Widow Tapp and her family settled into new quarters. Their cabin survived the battle but was mysteriously destroyed in 1865. A second cabin built in the same location was also destroyed years later. Each time, the family rebuilt.

Another widow, Permelia Higgerson, remarried in 1867, but she would find little happiness in her postwar life. She and her new husband, Daniel Porter, had two children, but

the youngest, a daughter, died as a teenager. Daniel, meanwhile, had an affair with his stepdaughter, Jacqueline. When Jacqueline eventually became pregnant, she and her stepfather ran off together to Missouri. Permelia, left behind, watched as the first of Daniel's children passed away, leaving behind two boys of his own. Their grandmother took them in.

When families like the Carpenters returned to their farms, they found the shallow graves of Union and Confederate soldiers.

Meanwhile, Permelia's brother, Absalom, tried for years on his mother's behalf to get compensation from the United States government for the damage done to their home at Mount View and property stolen from the farm. In 1875, Absalom's mother died, although Absalom continued to pursue the case, which was finally denied. Absalom eventually gave up and re-modeled the farmhouse on his own in 1891, and he lived there until his death in 1923. His former slave, Thorton, lived at Mount View, too, until his death sometime in the 1880s.

Absalom's family, which occupied Mount View until it burned down in 1947, continued to find artifacts from the war strewn across the property. Some leftovers were less innocuous than others: Parts of the Chewning farm remained off limits for years because of unexploded ordinance.

President Warren G. Harding, Marine Major General Smedley Butler, and Civil War veteran John Goolrick at the 1921 war games conducted by the Marines on the old Wilderness battlefield.

War of a kind returned to the Wilderness in the fall of 1921. More than four thousand Marines marched into the area for a four-day training exercise. Under the command of General Smedley Butler, the Marines outlined an imaginary battleship in the Wilderness Run valley, then used their planes and anti-aircraft guns and nighttime searchlights to "defend" the ship. President Warren Harding attended the event.

By then, life at nearby Ellwood had dramatically slowed. The Lacys had moved out of the big house, back to Fredericksburg, in the 1890s. In 1907, their children sold the property to Hugh Evander Willis, a respected legal scholar. Willis's family lived at Ellwood until 1977, when they turned the property over to the National Park Service.

But perhaps the real end of the postwar era came in June 1944. One of the Wilderness' oldest residents, the last-known civilian who survived the great battle of May 1864—four-year-old Eliza "Phenie" Tapp—died at the age of 84, just days before Allied forces stormed the beaches of Normandy in another, very different war. "Her death marks the removal of

one more link with the past," her obituary read; "one more living being who walked the same roads that Lee and Longstreet and Meade and Grant trod is now gone.

"She saw the same violets and bluets in that wood of death that the soldiers trampled underfoot and spattered with their blood. Now she and the soldiers are gone, but the flowers are the same every May, still blooming along the dusty 'plank' road and on the grass-covered trenches, while the adversaries of that battlefield, reincarnate in their descendants of a new century, fight now side by side."

Former National Park Service historian Ralph Happel (left) interviews "Phenie" Tapp (right), the last-known civilian survivor of the Battle of the Wilderness.

The National Park Service took possession of Ellwood in 1977. By then, the owners had sided the house with wooden shingles.

ABOUT THE AUTHOR

Chris Mackowski, an associate professor of journalism and mass communication at St. Bonaventure University, has won numerous awards for his writing. He is the co-author of *The Last Days of Stonewall Jackson* and *Chancellorsville: The Battle and the Battlefield,* as well as numerous Civil War articles. He works as a historical interpreter at Fredericksburg & Spotsylvania National Military Park.